PRAISE FOR
FUTURE WORSHIP

LaMar Boschman is a leader of integrity and a man of great passion for the presence of the Lord.

FRANK DAMAZIO
SENIOR PASTOR, CITY BIBLE CHURCH
PORTLAND, OREGON

LaMar Boschman helps us to see beyond the method to the meaning, beyond the music to the message of true worship. This is an important philosophical and practical work.

CHARLES V. SIMPSON
MOBILE, ALABAMA

I know of no one better qualified to analyze, evaluate and predict what worship in the Church will look like in the unfolding millennium.

BOB SORGE
AUTHOR, *EXPLORING WORSHIP* AND *IN HIS FACE*
LEE'S SUMMIT, MISSOURI

FUTURE WORSHIP

HOW A CHANGING WORLD CAN ENTER
GOD'S PRESENCE IN THE NEW MILLENNIUM

LaMar Boschman

Renew

A Division of Gospel Light
Ventura, California, U.S.A.

Published by Renew Books
A Division of Gospel Light
Ventura, California, U.S.A.
Printed in U.S.A.

Renew Books is a ministry of Gospel Light, an evangelical Christian publisher dedicated to serving the local church. We believe God's vision for Gospel Light is to provide church leaders with biblical, user-friendly materials that will help them evangelize, disciple and minister to children, youth and families.

It is our prayer that this Renew book will help you discover biblical truth for your own life and help you meet the needs of others. May God richly bless you.

For a free catalog of resources from Renew Books/Gospel Light please contact your Christian supplier or call 1-800-4-GOSPEL or at www.gospellight.com.

Cover Design by Kevin Keller
Interior Design by Rob Williams
Edited by William Simon

LIBRARY OF CONGRESS CATALOGING-IN-PUBLICATION DATA
Boschman, LaMar.
    Future worship / LaMar Boschman.
       p.   cm.
    Includes bibliographical references.
    ISBN 0-8307-2421-4 (pbk.)
    1. Public worship.   I. Title.
    BV15. B67   1999   99-13638
    264—dc21   CIP

1 2 3 4 5 6 7 8 9 10 11 12 13 14 15 / 05 04 03 02 01 00 99

Rights for publishing this book in other languages are contracted by Gospel Literature International (GLINT). GLINT also provides technical help for the adaptation, translation and publishing of Bible study resources and books in scores of languages worldwide. For further information, contact GLINT, P.O. Box 4060, Ontario, CA 91761-1003, U.S.A. You may also send E-mail to Glintint@aol.com or visit their website at www.glint.org.

I dedicate this book to three men who saw something on the horizon.

*My thanks to Rex Miller, whose inspiration and encouragement
to articulate what we saw for the future inspired me. This book would
not have been possible without your research and life work on the subject.*

*I want to acknowledge the tremendous help that Thomas Hohstadt was
to me in the preparation for this book. The hours of research and writing
helped tremendously.*

*Most of all I would like to thank Ed Chinn for his excellent writing
contribution that stated the vision of the future in a clear and positive
manner and brought the horizon closer.*

CONTENTS

Epilogue
Appendix

FOREWORD

If you are looking for a new book on worship that follows the predictable patterns of advocates of contemporary worship, that makes you feel good, and that gently settles you into your comfort zone—you have the wrong book in your hands! If you are looking for a critical, iconoclastic book on worship that breaks all the molds, that envelops you with major guilt complexes, and that leaves you upset with both God and the devil—you still have the wrong book in your hands!

Well, then, what do you have?

Future Worship is an incredibly important contribution to the Body of Christ in this hour. It is not another guidebook as to what you should do when your church meets next Sunday morning. Rather, it is a profound overview of the changing historical and cultural context in which we live. More importantly, this book is a beacon light pointing the direction we should collectively move in to keep the message of the gospel relevant to those around us. It is a book about worship, but much, much more than worship.

LaMar Boschman is among the most highly respected teachers in worship today. I have benefited greatly from his previous books; he has taught me as much about contemporary worship as anyone. As I read this book, however, I found myself learning more about the ways in which our culture is undergoing radical changes than I actually learned about worship itself. This book carries a message not just for worship leaders, but a message that all Christian leaders would do well to digest. Any pastor under 55 years of age who is not aware of the societal changes that LaMar analyzes so astutely in this book will be pastoring with one hand tied behind the back. Even pastors over 55 will greatly benefit.

I am over 55. When LaMar vividly describes the transitions from the print age to the electronic age to the digital age, I clearly see myself as a product of the print age. To use his imagery, I can more easily identify with Bob Dole than with Bill Clinton. For that reason alone, I could never get elected to a political office. To illustrate, I would much rather get my news through a newspaper or *Time* magazine than from television. Yes, I have become a bit conversant with the electronic age, but I am totally in another world when it comes to the digital age.

Why do I mention this? It is very simple. My generation is only a historical eyelash away from oblivion. But the Church will continue. Jesus is the same yesterday, today and forever. When I read a book like *Future Worship*, I am extremely encouraged. When my cohorts and I leave this world, the Body of Christ will be in good hands. God has raised up people like LaMar Boschman, who will not be left groping in a turbulent future characterized by radical and escalating changes. They understand what is happening and they know what to do about it. The gospel will be communicated in ways that it will be heard and understood. Jesus will continue to build His Church as He has for 2,000 years, and in it, whatever form or shape it might take, multitudes will still be worshiping the King of kings and the Lord of lords!

C. Peter Wagner
Wagner Leadership Institute

FOREWORD

True worship is unchanging. It is the outpouring of a person's soul/spirit unto the Triune God. From the beginning of creation through the entrance of the saints into eternity, worship remains intuitive to the redeemed spirit. We must worship someone, something, somehow. LaMar Boschman has made this crystal clear in his previous books.

Worship is enduring, but the styles of worship are ever changing. Culture, training, religious restraints, and even technology have formed, reformed, and transformed the way we worship. Boschman's book, *Future Worship,* chronicles these changes through the pages of Church history and reveals the changes that are now occurring in modern worship experiences.

Reading this book will make you uncomfortable at times. It will become a giant magnifying mirror that reveals pimples and scars on your face of worship. It will also identify areas of weakness in our present worship mode, especially here in America. What will make you even more uncomfortable is you know he is right. He gives vocabulary to what you have sensed inwardly.

The book, however, is not a witch hunt. It is less concerned with what is wrong than it is attentive to how we got here, and how we can go on to something greater. Boschman's projection of where he feels the worship experience will go in the future is insightful and seems to be right on target.

If he is correct, and I believe that he is, we will either make adjustments in our presentation of the worship experience, or we will end up with a ritual that is out of step with our changing culture.

Historically, the Church has always lagged behind culture changes. These changes are coming so rapidly these days that we dare not get too far behind the curve, or we will never catch up.

Dr. Judson Cornwall

PART I

ENDINGS AND BEGINNINGS

One of the primary challenges of life is coping with change. We live out our lives in continuous endings and beginnings. We are always letting go of something, constantly awakening to new shapes and sounds.

Just as there is, necessarily, an overlap between generations, so there is between the many endings and beginnings of ideas, technologies, paradigms and cultural assumptions. The overlap period is not easy; it contains the competing claims of both—the dying and the yet to be born—ages. According to political activist Antonio Gramsci, "in this interregnum, a great variety of morbid symptoms appear." Too many today are distracted by the morbid symptoms. They do not understand that we are in the midst of "the interval between the decay of the old and the formation of the new." All of this is certainly true of the Church and worship.

In part one, containing chapters one through five, we will try to look through eyes of faith at the dynamics of endings and beginnings, especially as they relate to the Church and worship.

At times that will require us to face reality about the morbidity. But, more important, it is my prayer that the examination will build our faith and confidence for the future. After all, Jesus' lordship includes the future!

In parts two and three, we will look at the new sounds and shapes in the future of worship.

THE INTERVAL BETWEEN THE DECAY OF THE OLD AND THE FORMATION AND THE ESTABLISHMENT OF THE NEW, CONSTITUTES A PERIOD OF TRANSITION WHICH MUST ALWAYS NECESSARILY BE ONE OF UNCERTAINTY, CONFUSION, ERROR, AND WILD FANATICISM.

—John C. Calhoun

CHAPTER ONE

COLLISION COURSE WITH REALITY

Jack Chinn was on board the *U.S.S. Princeton* when that new aircraft carrier was launched at the Philadelphia Naval Shipyard in 1942. For two and a half years, the ship was home to Chinn and several hundred other men. More than just a military vessel, the *Princeton* was also a small town. Naturally, the crew had a strong sense of community. Its citizenry included entrepreneurs, dreamers, pastors, alcoholics, losers, cops, cons, Christians and pagans. Lifelong friendships were forged in that floating village.

On October 24, 1944, life in the small town called *Princeton* changed forever. During the *Battle of Leyte Gulf*, a single bomb from a Japanese airplane hit the flight deck, exploded through the lower levels of the ship, and instantly killed many men. Within a few hours, the ship had slipped to the bottom of the sea, leaving hundreds of survivors adrift in an alien and dangerous environment. All of the familiar patterns of life were suddenly and irrevocably altered. The men had to develop new survival skills, adjust to new communal patterns, adapt new forms of communication (like waving articles of clothing at distant ships), and cope with new reasons, rhythms, and resources for living.

New communities formed in and around life rafts and floating debris. Men who had been antagonists, or perhaps never even met, were suddenly sharing a life-sustaining piece of the wooden flight deck. Men from very diverse operational units found themselves thrown together into the brand-new neighborhood of a life raft.

Chinn's eyes dance and his face breaks into a large smile when he recalls, "First thing we did in our life raft was call a prayer meeting. We all began to call on God. Some were repentin' and others were just sobbin' as they cried out to the Lord, a few just kinda mumbled. But, we were all sincere and determined to get holda God."

Chinn goes on to describe one particular shipmate. "Even ole' Swede—he was the roughest, meanest, cussinest man on the ship; and he said to the rest of us, 'Now, men, let's all look right up at God and just pour our hearts out to Him. Now, I mean it, let's all tell 'im we're sorry for our sinnin' and that we need help.'"

Today, more than a half century later, Chinn remembers, "You know, I've been in a lotta church services and prayer meetin's over the past seventy years. But the best service I ever attended was in that life raft in the South Pacific."[1]

Being an authority on church worship, Chinn's story provokes me because his life-raft service begs one simple question: What church model was that, anyway?

THE "HELP! MY SHIP IS SUNK" CHURCH MODEL

Where did the format—the liturgy—of the service in the life raft come from? Was that a *seeker-sensitive, purpose-driven, permission-*

giving, twenty-first-century, or *new-apostolic* group? What motivational gifting test helped "ole' Swede" find his ministry of teaching "the Body" how to pray?

Is it possible that one Japanese bomb may have led more people to Christ than many churches and evangelistic events do today?

Could it be that current weather catastrophes and global convulsions actually reflect "the riches of His grace, which He lavished upon us" (Eph. 1:7,8)? Imagine, at the spoken word of God, natural forces taking hold of the borders of the earth and producing results far beyond the power of any human agency! God revealed much about His activity in the earth when He asked Job,

> Have you ever in your life commanded the morning, and caused the dawn to know its place; That it might take hold of the ends of the earth, and the wicked be shaken out of it? (Job 38:12,13).

God knows how to motivate people to run into His house and into His arms. Through external pressures, setbacks and difficulties, people flock to a loving Creator for safety and sustenance. Charles Simpson observed how in Psalm 27, King David would seek God when he recognized that various "adversaries" and "evildoers" were intent on his destruction (vv. 2,3 *KJV*). Although under the threat of enemies overtaking him, David suddenly proclaims, "One thing have I desired of the Lord, that will I seek after; that I may dwell in the house of the Lord all the days of my life" (v. 4).

What a contrast for many of us today. We often wring our hands, scratch our heads and stare at world events with perplexity. We wonder why things have jumped out of control. Yet, is God really wringing *His* hands about history—about us? Why do we assume that history is like a big bus lunging through crowded streets and playgrounds with a dead driver at the wheel? Do we truly believe that we serve One who is powerless in the face of out of control circumstances on earth?

One could argue that the global convulsions are doing a good job at motivating people to grope for God. There are millions of seekers (prompted by unexpected problems and tragedies) desperately searching for the meaning of life. They're looking for reality in various philosophies, religions, cults, psychics, palm readers, technologies and New Age beliefs. The harvest has begun.

However, the Church seems to be either threatened by, or ignorant of, the significance of these changing times. It is often defensive, angry and fearful. And, while the "contractions of history" are squeezing millions into a quest for truth, the Church is largely preoccupied with polarization politics, special interest groups, anger, and trying to raise funds to pay for property and programs that have nothing to do with the harvest.

As a result, many seekers eliminate the Church as a serious contender for being a life source. These seekers conclude the Church does not care about them. Moreover, these people even argue that the Christian Body suffers a serious break with reality.

What constitutes reality? There are two components—actual substance and our experience with it. All of us are vulnerable to the illusions that come from confusing our own perceptions with objective reality. That is the essence of a pharisaical attitude and it grows especially well in the hothouses of religious culture. This appears whenever language evokes a reality that is subverted by behavior. Jesus told the Pharisees of His day, "You have a fine way of setting aside the commands of God in order to observe your own traditions!" Jesus essentially said to them and the Pharisees in every age, "You want the truth? You can't handle the truth!"

Unable or unwilling to handle the truth, the Church has turned away from reality and become narcissistic. Glen Roachelle, president of Gate Ministries, has been in Christian ministry over 35 years and has watched this narcissism grow. As a pastor, church planter and church consultant, he has extensive and knowledgeable experience in various church cultures across the United States. He makes a distinction between the biblical concept of the Church and the contemporary version of it ("the visible Church") in American society.

He believes that spiritual narcissism has led the contemporary and visible church "to pine away in love for its own image. She thinks she's rich and in need of nothing. She does not see that she has become fundamentally self-indulgent and, worse, is blind to her deeply dysfunctional state. She does not realize she has been seduced away from the simplicity that is in Christ Jesus. She is now in love with herself, and cannot see the Lord for looking into the pool of Narcissus."[2]

Futurist Rex Miller has pointed out that "truth is only the seed of the reality that it promises. It can't survive soil that has been eroded away by past fads that run through organizations and cultures like flash floods. It doesn't do well in soil burned out by overuse and abuse. Truth requires good soil. So maybe the failure rates we have experienced are more of a reflection on the condition of the soil than on the truth."[3]

Now, when I hear thoughtful and provocative words like that, one part of me protests, *Come on, guys, the Church is the last best hope for a **society** that can't handle the truth.* But even I have to admit that the Church seems

VANITY'S A DEADLY SIN. IT'S WHAT THE FLESH IS PACKAGED IN.
—BLUE OYSTER CULT

deeply flawed in its capacity to allow the transformational quality of truth inside.

BRIAN'S SONG

Brian started out as a typical teenager. Born in Canton, Ohio, Brian's father was a hard-working furniture salesman; the family went to church. But Brian's lanky appearance and poor health made him an eventual target for teasing and mocking by schoolmates. Without his dad there as a coach and mentor, Brian had to face a barrage of ridicule and chastisement all alone.

When Brian's father was home, he would tyrannize Brian when anything was wrong or out of order. Sometimes the only attention Brian received from his father was a belt slapped across his backside. Brian lived in fear of his father and felt that he was worthless and would never amount to anything.

In 1974, Brian's parents enrolled him in a Christian School where he received years of religious instruction through Bible studies, movies and discussions on the impending "apocalypse." He was often afraid that the world would come to an end and he wouldn't go to heaven. He was terrified by the idea of the Antichrist and the end of the world.

Brian often thought, *What if I already have the mark of the beast? What if the Antichrist is inside of me?*

It was more than he could handle. Not only was he going through puberty and all the questions and fears brought into his life by those dynamics; now he had to cope with the weight of eschatological judgment and destruction. His Christian culture did a job on Brian about the "end-times." His nightmares were frequent and horrendous. To this day, Brian cannot sleep without the television on or some noise to reassure him.

Brian felt that he stood out from the other students; he didn't respond to altar calls like the rest of his peers. He was too afraid to stand in front of the whole Christian School and admit that he was morally and spiritually inferior to everyone else. The teachers were pressuring him to conform to their culture and beliefs. He was often scolded and sometimes considered blasphemous.

"I tried to fit into their idea of Christianity, to prove my connection with their beliefs, and all I received was punishment for it," he said. When he was cast as Jesus in a school play about the crucifixion, some students ripped off the loincloth Brian was wearing. Naked and humiliated, he was then chased and beaten in front of other students, too.

Brian developed very pronounced and intense opinions about Christians from those experiences. Today, he has nothing kind to say about them. He paints his face white and colors his lips black, accenting his long jet-black hair. Dark eye shadow sets surreal eyes deep into his face. His fishnet stockings and short shirt barely cover the scars of self-mutilation, a common practice among those that are emotionally tormented. Brian's body piercing and strange tattoos finish his look of revenge. He wants to shock the Christians that forced their dogma and rules on him and never loved him.

Brian Warner of Canton, Ohio, grew up to be Marilyn Manson.

Now, at last, he feels accepted and has a sense of pride when he sings of his pain and hatred—acceptance and pride he never felt in the Church or in a Christian school.

"I want to become what adults fear the most!"

Tens of thousands of postmodern Gen-Xers can relate to Brian. These kids feel unaccepted and forced into obeying rules from a culture that cares little for their fashion and tastes. So they work hard to shock Christians—the Church—the establishment.

Manson becomes a messenger for them as he portrays evil and hatred. What is the message? "You do not understand and do not love us; you cannot connect or relate."

"In many ways my desire is actually to be pure again and not dirtied by the world. But I felt it's my duty to be as ugly and filthy as I am...so the audience can experience what I've experienced. It's cathartic," Manson admits.[4]

Walt Mueller, in is his article on Manson in *New Man* magazine said, "Even Manson is reacting not to biblical Christianity, but to the distorted, Americanized version of Christianity common in today's American churches."[5]

How do we relate to Brian's culture? How would Jesus connect with him?

> God was in Christ reconciling the world to Himself, not counting their trespasses against them, and He has committed to us the word of reconciliation (2 Cor. 5:19).

Marilyn Manson gives the Church a window of how to connect with people who want help but who do not want a dead and suffocating religion. His "compatibility" with religious paradigms and cultures is not the issue; his very real concerns and confusions are! But some say, "He is so, uh, *different*." But that very difference is the window. Now there is a wider spectrum of "different" out in the world than the Church has ever seen, and a greater and stranger vista of *different* is coming in the future. How are we ever going to reach them with the word of reconciliation if we blow it with the Marilyn Mansons?

In fact, the future is going to require the Church to humble herself, repent of her narcissism, and embrace the word of reconciliation. Let's face it: God is not even counting full-blown sin, let alone tattoos and pierced body parts!

Why is the Church so distracted from (or ignorant of) the real purpose of "the contractions of history"? We should be positioned to catch the (harvest) baby. Instead, we're wandering around in various states of bewilderment, vertigo, disillusionment, anger, narcissism, and just plain goofiness.

What freak mutations of classic Christianity are we generating?

ILLUSIONS

I believe the Church is the Bride of Christ. But I also agree with Charles Simpson who said, "The Church is Christ's Bride, but she's not His whole life!" Godly men cherish, honor and enjoy their wives. We would die for them. However, a quick survey of a man's life will reveal that a relatively small portion of his work and pursuits are concentrated on his wife. The Church's collision course with reality is a reflection of her illusion that she is His whole life. *The Kingdom of God is His life. She's His wife.*

AN ERA CAN BE SAID TO END WHEN ITS BASIC ILLUSIONS ARE EXHAUSTED.

—ARTHUR MILLER

The Church is *part* of His kingdom. But it is not synonymous with the Kingdom!

I am positive about the future, including the future of the Church. I wholeheartedly agree with Loren B. Mead that "We are at the front edges of the greatest transformation of the church...it may eventually make the transformation of the Reformation look like a ripple in a pond."[6] Yet I believe that a glorious future for the Church will follow a revelation about the difference between the Kingdom and the Church. The Church will exhaust her illusions about her role and find a new sense of perspective on her relationship to Him and a new understanding about the scope of His work.

If an era comes to an end when its basic illusions are exhausted, as playwriter Arthur Miller suggests, then the Church is surely in that "overlap" period between two eras—one in decline and one that's emerging. The purpose of this book is to identify the character and markings of a new era in church worship—the "crown jewel of the Church." However, before we can apprehend the features of the new age, we must face reality about the dying one.

This is a changing era saturated by several unhealthy perceptions—illusions—that have squelched the true nature of church and worship.

1. THE CHURCH AS A BUILDING OR EVENT

Christians often identify the Church as being a physical structure or a tangible event rather than a spiritual structure focused on loving God and one's neighbor. This preoccupation with the physical realm is a materialist assumption—an illusion—rooted in the past with no credibility in a post-materialist future.

A decade ago, independent researcher and technology writer George Gilder wrote, "The central event of the twentieth century is the overthrow of matter. In technology, economics, and the politics of nations, wealth in the form of physical resources is declining...Finally, the overthrow of matter will stultify all materialist philosophy and open new vistas of human imagination and moral revival."[7]

Gilder recognized that we are in the midst of a social upheaval involving the use of new technological mediums for communication. These changes will force Christians to see the Church as more than a glorified structure or a hyped audio-video event. The current explosion of information and communication allows people to interact with one another without ever meeting in a building or congregating for a scheduled affair.

As a worship leader, I know that many Christians consider the Church to be event-driven. Too often, we gather for an event experience, but we don't know how to simply relate and interact with other members of the Lord's Body. It is very possible that our leaving this age dominated by materialistic thought may take us back to a more relational era when people just talked to one another; when they spoke through the simple, God-given means of words, facial expressions and posture that communicated accurately what was in their hearts.

In the following chapters, we will examine how communication technology may be a Spirit-birthed instrument of "the overthrow of matter" as an assumption and basis for the Church.

2. THE SEARCH FOR THE "RIGHT" CHURCH MODEL

One of the reasons that we know we are living in a declining era is because we are so saturated by so many different church models and paradigms; we have seeker-driven churches, purpose-driven churches, permissive churches, resurrected churches, twenty-first-century churches, metro metamorphosis-size churches and new apostolic churches, just to mention a few.

Brian D. McLaren reminds us that "The most celebrated and notoriously successful models as I write—Bill Hybels, Rick Warren and John Maxwell for example—became successful through bold innovation and creative synthesis, not through unthinking imitation...truly successful models earned their success the old-fashioned way—through pain, tears, endurance, mistakes, and prayer...If you imitate them as successful models, whatever kind of success you get probably won't be the kind they got."[8]

There is a reason that Jack Chinn remembers the service in the life raft as the best he ever attended; God is perfectly capable of imparting really good models for church and worship!

3. EXTERNAL CIRCUMSTANCES OVER ETERNAL TRUTHS

Those who sail the seas are sensitive to the weather. Only a foolish sailor resents adverse sailing conditions; wise ones assume them. Local churches are much like sailing ships on oceanic voyages. Their loyalty is always to the flag dancing at the top of their mast and their goal is the destination port, but they live as if governed by the wind of circumstances and currents of the day.

Only moronic sailors protest the howling wind, reminisce about yesterday's placid waters, or spiritualize the storm. Such would be considered a stupid and lethal drain of valuable energy (but real sailors would probably describe it in language far more colorful and earthy than that!).

However, the contemporary church is obsessed by the wind. We pray against the social issue winds, we grow sentimental about the calm winds and waters of "the old days," we try to derive spiritual lessons (and sermon material) from every breeze. We also take our bearings from the wind of events and not from our compass— God's truth and presence—that always points true north.

4. ENCULTURATION MISTAKEN FOR PURITY

The disconnection with the presence of God is creating spiritual ghettos in the contemporary Church, and this disconnection is rooted, I believe, in a basic self-righteousness. Its moralism has created the illusion (suggested by Jacques Ellul in chapter 2) that the Church is not part of society and is, somehow, free from the sin of the world.

However, the tenacity of the illusion has created a sanctimonious isolation from the real world. We remain in ghettos. We still feel threatened and challenged by the real world, by "the different." We are often in our own little world like the crew members of an airliner; we have no idea what is going on in the lives of passengers who briefly occupy the seats (pews) in our isolated little world. We do not "mix" with them out of fear of contamination. We are just "company men," loyal to an illusion of "purity" and forgetting that we exist to serve the passengers and help them connect with their destination and purpose. Because of our self-righteousness and moralism, we so often ignore the call of God to touch the suffering, the sinful, the poor and the diseased.

Just one look at Christian television and it is obvious that our attitudes, words, dress, and ideas are outdated and even dangerous. So much of the contemporary Church is increasingly a museum of anthropology. It represents a crystallized, antiquated, ineffective, even humorous display of a way of life that has not existed in years. No wonder my new neighbors politely chuckled when they heard I am a minister.

Normal people may want to occasionally visit a museum; they surely do not want to live there! Seekers today want reality; they don't want to sit and stare at a taxidermy of a prehistoric beast. Seekers are hungry. They want some answers, and the seeker wants God. Often all we have to offer them is a program, a song list, or best sermon of the week.

5. SUPERFICIALITY

For various reasons, the Church is too often an enclave of unreality. I think we've all grown weary of the plastic smiles, empty questions, and dishonest responses. The weird thing is that everyone knows such exchanges are empty and dishonest! Someone says, "How are you doing?" Our response is: "Great, great; filled with faith and power"—the way religion teaches us to say. Perhaps we should be honest: "My heart is broken, I'm lonely, and I don't think I can tolerate my boss, my kids, or you for another minute."

In any system characterized by unreality, externals and perceptions are essential while internals and truth are secondary.

Many churches become gatherings of abstract nonpersons—those who come to see the program and do not know how to get real or close to others attending. So, people tend to develop holograms of themselves. They present the holograms rather than the real thing. Ever try to reach inside a hologram? You grab the same thing that you would in conversation with most religious people—air!

Unreality and superficiality—the holographic illusion—is perhaps the most representative mark of an age that is dying.

Sally Morgenthaler wrote in her book, *Worship Evangelism*, "Many people have had enough. They have had their fill of superficial, human-centered services, and they simply are not going to take it anymore. Some may still come to church to hear comedy routines and watch 'the show,' but increasing numbers do not—they come to meet with God."[9] And Chuck Lofy says, "When the church is no longer transparent to the divine and people don't feel the presence of God, they will drift...."[10]

It seems to me that much of the Church is hungry for some meat and potatoes. Youth do not want to be babysat, adults want some definite answers, and the seeker wants God. People are increasingly hungry for the presence of God. Where is God in our services? Do we give Him a hologram every morning? How can we connect better with the presence of Jesus?

I think Os Guinness has captured the superficiality of the dying age perfectly:

Having visited almost all the countries in the English-speaking world, I would say that I know none where the churches are more full and the sermons more empty than in America. There are magnificent exceptions, of course. By and large, I am never hungrier and rarely angrier than when I come out of an American

Evangelical church after what passes for the preaching of the Word of God. The problem is not just the heresy, though doubtless there is some of that. Nor is it just the degree of entertainment, and there is lots of that. Nor is it even the appalling gaps in the theology, for there is far too much of that. The real problem is that in what is said there is almost no sense of announcement from God; and in what is shown there is almost no sense of anointing by God.[11]

No Sense of Announcement from God; No Sense of Anointing by God

Guinness provides the perfect tombstone for the church age that is ending. For if the Church carries no announcement and operates with no anointing, it is useless. But rather than dwell on *What Went Wrong*, the purpose of this book is an attempt to catch glimpses of a more glorious future.

> It is already the hour for you to awaken from sleep; for now salvation is nearer to us than when we believed. The night is almost gone, and the day is at hand (Rom. 13:11,12).

I do believe the night is almost gone and a new era is dawning. It is nearer than many of us believe.

As I travel throughout the United States and around the globe, I am seeing that more leaders are crying out for help. They are also awakening to the reality that the church of the dying age cannot be fixed. They are moving beyond traditionalism and sentimentality. They are straining to catch the first rays of the dawn.

When we speak of the Church we are actually speaking of two very different things. One is eternal and mysterious. It will never be understood because it is the Body of Christ. The other is the temporal, cultural institution that grows up around the eternal. The former is ever glorious; the latter always crystallizes and dies.

The eternal and mysterious Church will grow in unlikely places. It can be expressed through various sects, fellowships, ministries and individuals in all races, nations, generations and denominations. There are Christian's who worship in Mormon temples, Catholic cathedrals, Protestant churches and Islamic mosques. Yes, in all these places there are individuals who have a relationship with Jesus Christ and, together, they express His Body in the earth. The kingdom of God is within them.

However, when we typically refer to the Church, we mean that institution where religion has eclipsed and even obliterated relationship. Rules, rituals and rites have given different groups of the Church their identity. Politics, programs and personalities have dictated what was to occur in the Christian's public worship service. Doctrine, dogma and darkness have separated us into small ghettos. Much of the Body of Christ has been seduced and segregated by opportunists and spells of personalities.

But the fact remains that the Church is Christ's Bride, His love and delight. He is returning for her. He is not returning for the institutions, fellowships, buildings, societies, ministries and events that we often call the Church.

It's time for all Christians to grow up and realize that the temporal, cultural institution we call the Church is on a collision course with reality. But an equally sure (and far more glorious) reality is that the eternal Church will "morph" into new shapes and patterns and will connect in new ways with the needs of the world for which Christ died.

Notes

1. Jack Chinn, telephone interview by Ed Chinn, n.d.
2. Ibid.
3. Rex Miller, "All Things New" (unpublished work), n.d, n.p.
4. *Details* (Dec., 1996), n.p.
5. Walt Mueller, "Marilyn Manson's Revenge" *New Man* (Sept./Oct. 1998), p. 35.
6. Loren B. Mead, *The Once and Future Church* (Bethesda, MD: The Alban Institute, 1991), p. 68.
7. George Gilder, *Microcosm* (New York: Simon & Schuster, 1989), pp. 17, 18.
8. Brian D. McLaren, *Reinventing Your Church* (Grand Rapids, MI: Zondervan Publishing House, 1998), pp. 113, 114.
9. Sally Morgenthaler, *Worship Evangelism* (Grand Rapids, MI: Zondervan Publishing House, 1995), p. 24.
10. Chuck Lofy, taped presentation, "The Voices of Change," Changing Church for a Changing World Conference, Prince of Peace Lutheran Church, Burnsville, MN, April 1993.
11. Os Guinness, *The Devil's Gauntlet* (Downers Grove, IL: InterVarsity Press, 1989), n.p.

CHAPTER TWO

ARE THE GOOD TIMES GONE?

Chances are you got this book through a Christian source. Perhaps you bought it from a Christian bookstore or book club; maybe you received it as a gift from a pastor, worship leader or other Christian friend. Whatever the source, it is pretty safe—just because of the realities of marketing and distribution—to assume that it came out of some spigot along that Christian distribution pipeline.

That very maze of filters and faucets may actually prevent you from understanding it. Why? Because Christians (like any other group) tend to perceive truth through the inculcated cultural screens developed from their own traditions, assumptions and structures. Most groups eventually crystallize into disjointed, incoherent and narcissistic navel gazers. Contemporary Christians are not exempt from that apparent inevitability. We tend to view everything through that narrow keyhole of how it relates to my church and my belief system.

TROUBLE RIGHT HERE IN RIVER CITY

Pastor Harold was just stepping out of the shower as Joyce called him to breakfast. He knew he was running late for the early service so he quickly towel-dried, wrapped his loins in that enormous beach towel they bought in Biloxi, and went sliding into the bright sunflower-and-blue-gingham kitchen. As Joyce poured his coffee, he picked up the remote and shot a beam to the TV.

The lead story on the local Sunday morning news program seized Harold and Joyce's full attention.

Avery Pinkston, a local barber and beauty supply salesman, had kidnapped the 14-year-old daughter of a very prominent industrialist. He had threatened to rape and kill her if he didn't get $200,000. The money drop had been made in a plastic Winn-Dixie bag, near the shrub in the median in front of the Taco Bell as requested. Avery himself was arrested when he scooped it up and went roaring away in his '89 Dodge Caravan. He was being held without bond. His wife told officers that he was a good husband and father, but that "he was just crazy" because of a bad check he'd written to a casino in Atlantic City.

HE CAUSES HIS SUN TO RISE ON THE EVIL AND THE GOOD. AND SENDS RAIN ON THE RIGHTEOUS AND UNRIGHTEOUS.

—MATTHEW 5:45

The pastor stood, mouth open, water dripping from his hair. He looked at the kitchen clock, turned to Joyce and groaned, "Dear Jesus, it's almost eight o'clock; how can we ever find someone at this hour to teach Avery's Sunday School class?"

Hit in the face with the icy waters of human tragedy, we Christians tend to perceive only the details which relate to our own very small reality. Therefore, we tend to think and act like Pastor Harold. Most of us have lived in the Christian ghetto for so long that we have little cognizance that we are actually part of a larger world. Obviously, we are not prepared or equipped to deal with it.

In *The Presence of the Kingdom*, Jacques Ellul reminded us that Christians are "part of the whole body of humankind" and therefore a Christian "cannot declare that he is free from the sin of the world."[1] So here we are, fixed by gravity to the same planet, breathing the same air and drinking the same water, and living in the same culture as other "earthlings." Yet we somehow have found and embraced an idea that we do not share in a basic commonality. We think in an "us versus them" mentality; we are simply "better" than they. We are proud and self-centered.

How did we who call ourselves Christians develop such an un-Christian (and just plain goofball) idea?

Author and social commentator Don Eberly answers that question by pointing out the detachment of most Christians from the very world that God loves and for which Christ died.

The Christian voice in America is ineffective because it has not been disciplined or sharpened by serious encounters with the secular world. The vast majority of Christians in America are unwilling or unprepared to engage the secular, except to regularly make it the object of their protest. The difference between Christian leadership in the past and the present is that we once acknowledged the fact that evil lurks within all our hearts, yes even Christian hearts, which is why our starting point in engaging the world must be an attitude of forgiveness and humility.

I ask you, is there even a biblical basis for Christians fighting in their own defense? Yet we have a solid record of defending ourselves, while our defense of others does not extend much beyond the unborn. When did you last hear of an Evangelical Christian defending others— African Americans, Jews, Muslims and other ethnics— when they've been attacked or maligned? Why is it that we Christians so loathe our world and our unredeemed neighbors? Is it because we believe that our sovereign God's only purpose in history is rescuing the redeemed? We've completely lost such notions as natural law and common grace.[2]

TIME TO GET OUT OF THE GHETTO

Brian D. McLaren, pastor of Cedar Ridge Community Church in Burtonsville, Maryland, challenges the typical Christian insularity in his fine book, *Reinventing Your Church.*

To dismiss Buddhism when all Buddhists lived on the other side of the world was easy; but when a Buddhist lives next door or teaches your college chemistry class and proves to be a very good neighbor or professor, his or her beliefs are not so easily dismissed. To caricature all Muslims as terrorists is easy until you meet a Muslim of grace and ethical depth...we will have to stop giving ourselves permission to be prejudiced and stereotypical about members of other religions. We can't keep comparing our best with their worst and feeling smug.[3]

I really want to help you break out of the Christian ghetto and gain a larger view of God and His world. So, for starters, let me suggest that you read this book simply as a human being, an "earthling." If you are a Christian, try to read it more as a believer than a church member.

The real issues are not religious or even Christian. They are about life.

Life is a mystery. It originates in, and flows out from, God. When life appears on earth, it is always the result of the Creator touching His creation. That touch—His fingerprint—may produce a baby, release tears of forgiveness, inspire a song, build a romance, launch a friendship, give revelation (for a cotton gin, a silicon chip, a novel, or a spiritual truth), or create a vast array of other creations. Heaven touches earth and when the dust settles, an impartation of *life* has changed the landscape of a womb, a mountain, a heart or a community.

MAYBE IT'S TIME WE GOT BACK TO THE BASICS OF LIFE.

—WAYLON JENNINGS

Life is *organic;*[4] it is dynamic, volatile, unpredictable. It erupts, pulsates and procreates. It is, in fact, a *radical* existence; the word "radical" comes from a Latin word meaning "root."[5] A radical life is lived with its taproot in Jesus. A radical response is that which drills down through the layers of rubble to bore into the Aquifer of Life.

People are drawn to life. Whether they are black or white, hetero- or homosexual, pro-lifers or pro-choicers, boomers or Gen-Xers, Democrats or Republicans, reggae or rock lovers, Baptists or Buddhists, the human spirit will always search out the scent of water. People do not gravitate toward meetings, guilt trips, institutions, titles, traditions, or OPVs (other people's viewpoints). But they will always surge over the banks of national borders, economic constrictions or sociological boundaries—*just to get to a life source*!

For some reason, recipients of life seem to eventually feel the need to *control* that mystery; it just has to be dissected, analyzed and controlled. That process ultimately becomes so complicated that there is an extensive proliferation of traditions, rules and codes (designed, presumably, to "fire my imagination" about the mystery). Finally, the regulations and customs that were designed to interpret and enhance life begin to replace it; layers of interpretations must interpret earlier versions of interpretations. Then, just as numerous generations of audio recordings distort the original sound, the multiplied interpretations of truth tend to warp our perception of the sounds emanating out of eternal reality.

Ultimately, a complex, knotted, sticky web of opinions, injunctions and "useless information" becomes *institutionalized* between God and man. Life becomes crystallized into formalities, traditions smother light, spirit turns to law and the law starts handing out death certificates.

USELESS
INFORMATION
SUPPOSED TO
FIRE MY
IMAGINATION.

—MICK JAGGER AND
KEITH RICHARDS

DIVORCED FROM GOD'S PRESENCE

No wonder we "can't get no satisfaction." The power lines are down.

Simply stated, we are suffering an unprecedented degree of severance. Our cultural institutions, leaders, communities, families and individuals are disconnected from their classic—transcendent—sources and, therefore, are becoming *unstuck* from one another.

Maybe you've noticed...

You remember when piling into the car for a school or civic meeting was a normal part of your life? Do you remember the normalcy of regularly getting together with neighbors or coworkers for backyard cookouts or pool parties? Remember when it wasn't difficult to attend a public event?

Do you remember when "going to church" was easy? Sunday mornings—even Sunday and Wednesday evenings—were like cool, grassy paths that led naturally and effortlessly down to a *place* that was a symbol of the sweet and beautiful presence of God and the life-affirming fellowship of dear friends. The closer you got to the time and the place, you experienced an almost Pavlovian response of a rising anthem of praise in your heart, a near-physical hunger for the word of God, and the just-about-giddy anticipation of seeing friends.

WHAT HAPPENED?

Why do so many now feel spiritually homeless? Why do so many no longer go to any place called "church"? Why do we (those who still try to go at all) dread Sunday mornings? Why would we rather nail our tongues to a tree than go to a church meeting on a Wednesday night? Come to think of it, why are there so few church services on *any* night in America?

Do you remember when worship was worship? You could feel it springing up from your heart before you ever got there. It flowed from a grateful and adoring heart toward the One who rescued you from a futile way of life. It blew across your vocal chords and came flowing out your mouth (usually in the car on the way to the assembly). You could almost hear a heavenly choir beginning what would soon be joined by the folks you hung out with.

Today, worship is too often a cacophonous, raucous, aerobic dance class. People stand on platforms and command you to do stuff that you would *never* do in any rational moment of your life...like turning to the total stranger next to you and screaming, MY NAME IS BRADLEY AND I'M A JESUS POWER RANGER!

Christians seem to be living in a bubble of unreality. I guess that when the power lines are down, people adapt weird practices just to keep warm.

BOWLING ALONE

Consider this: All of the indices of civic and community participation, like church attendance, voter turnout, and other measurements of group life are in decline. It used to be easy and natural to go to gatherings. It was once a personally invigorating experience to engage and entertain neighbors, coworkers and other friends.

However, far fewer people spend any time with their neigh- bors, go to church, attend public events, or involve themselves in any other forms of community relationship than what was once considered part of the normal course of life.

Harvard Professor Robert Putnam has, for several years, been examining some of the basic indicators of community life in America. Putnam discovered that the number of Americans who attend a "public meeting on town or school affairs within the past year" had fallen 41 percent in the 25 years between 1973 and 1993. His research also revealed that participation in the electoral process, church attendance, organizational membership and "socializing with one's neighbors" have all experienced similar patterns of decline within the same twenty-year period.

One of Putnam's most interesting measurements of community life was bowling statistics: "More Americans are bowling today than ever before, but bowling in organized leagues has plummeted in the last decade or so. Between 1980 and 1993 the total number of bowlers in America increased by 10 percent, while league bowling decreased by 40 percent."

The inescapable conclusion of the bowling data is, of course, that recreation in America has, like other community life indices, become more private, less communal. In fact, Professor Putnam condenses his study with a wonderfully understated summary: "The best available evidence suggests that we are less connected with one another."[6] We are bowling by ourselves.

WHAT'S GOING ON HERE?

Various factors have contributed to our "disconnectivity"—suburbanization, busyness, the movement of women into the labor force, increased mobility, divorce, and shifting economic patterns. A few decades ago, it was widely predicted that future advances in technology would produce shorter periods of work, more leisure time, and earlier retirements. Today, the average American husband and wife work a combined total of nearly one hundred hours per week. In our own lifetime, I've heard we spend a total of eight months opening junk mail and *two years* unsuccessfully trying to reach people on the phone! I think it is arguably accurate to say that the advances in technology, particularly in communication, have made life far more complicated and busy.

However, all of these "usual suspects" may be more symptomatic of a larger reality.

Perhaps our *horizontal* disconnect is related to a *vertical* power outage. It seems as if a cosmic electromagnet once pulled people to certain alliances, institutions and activities; there was a noticeable gravitational force that made it easy to visit with neighbors, participate in school functions, or go to church. Today, it feels like the electromagnet has become disconnected. The power is off. So, traditionally adherent "particles" are drifting away. Moreover, new ones are not being pulled toward it. Therefore, many institutions and traditions are in a serious state of decline.

One of the great mysteries of anthropology relates to how civilizations simply vanish. For example, what happened to the Mayans of Central America? Why did these people—who had developed a perpetually correct calendar and understood the concept of zero a thousand years before anyone else did—simply disappear? And what caused Native Americans to carve out a 200-room palace in a mountain and then, after 1,200 years of civilization, vanish without a trace?

One of the most intriguing theories—and it is just a theory—explaining the total disappearance of these rather sophisticated and enduring civilizations is that they simply walked away. The theory postulates that all of the compelling reasons and rhythms for community life finally expired. Then, over time, the people just drifted away, perhaps into isolation or even to be integrated into other groups.

Whatever happened to them, this much is clear: Occasionally certain historical periods—including their great ideas, technologies, forms, myths, songs, traditions and all other cultural expressions—simply pass away. They perish and new ages emerge.

ENDINGS AND BEGINNINGS

Thou, Lord, in the beginning didst lay the foundation of the earth, and the heavens are the works of Thy hands; They will perish, but Thou remainest; and they all will become old as a garment, And as a mantle Thou wilt roll them up; as a garment they will also be changed. But Thou art the same, and Thy years will not come to an end (Heb. 1:10-12).

Is it possible that from time to time in the course of human history, God—through the utility of cosmic forces—simply folds up an entire age like a worn-out garment and lays it away somewhere?

Yes.

In fact, the One who created the universe and all of its features has also set its boundaries (see Ps. 74:16,17). Therefore, it is reasonable to conclude that ages always have, and will, come to an end and always were, and will be, succeeded by new ones just as glorious. Of course, the reality which makes that turbulent and perpetual change navigable is that He remains the same!

It is a simple truth: Ages begin and end; they come and they go. This is a simple truth, but the ramifications are the substance from which revolutions and realignments are made. The Bible refers to the wisdom of a declining age (see 1 Cor. 2:6). Each age has a characteristic set of assumptions, expectations and parameters. They serve *that* age; they are not eternal.

Ages don't end and begin in strict sequential order. Rather they overlap, like Olympic circles (see Figure 1). The period within the overlapping circles (the "football") holds the dynamics of an epic struggle, the competing demands and loyalties of the *old* and the *new*. Throughout history, these have been wrenching periods; times when the old was fighting to survive and the new was striving to be born. For example, the 1860s represented both the declining epoch of slavery and the emerging age of emancipation. The conflict between the two ages was so sharp that it produced the Civil War. The war was not between two parts of a country as much as it was between two ages.

Here, on the edge of a new millennium, we are living in another overlap

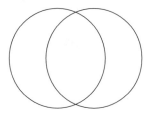

FIGURE 1

era. An old order is dying; a new one is being born. Once again, the "battle" is not between political philosophies, ethnic groups, theologies, socioeconomic groups, generations or any cultural details; it is a conflict between dominant paradigms from a dying age and an emerging one.

Fidel Castro was right when he said, "A revolution is not a bed of roses. A revolution is a struggle between the future and the past." Epic struggles between ages are always traumatic; seismic ruptures split the earth open, economies convulse, national borders collapse, there are floods and droughts, and people die. "Nation will rise against nation, and kingdom against kingdom; there will be earthquakes in various places; there will also be famines. These things are merely the beginning of the birth pangs" (Mark 13:8).

LET ALL THE DREAMERS WAKE THE NATION. COME, THE NEW JERUSALEM.

—CARLY SIMON

Let's face it—the global seismic activity will, in all likelihood, continue for a while; our traditions, assumptions and structures will continue to be assaulted; the indices of national life will keep on falling; the visible form of the Church will continue its slow roll into the dirt (like Jimmy Cagney taking 200 feet to die).

However, this writhing, throbbing demise will not change or threaten any eternal certainties. These birth pangs will take place under the watchful and vigilant care of our very confident Lord. Even the psalmist, after musing over the ever close presence of death, declares the faithfulness of God. "But Thou art the same, and Thy years will not come to an end" (Ps. 102:27).

Of course, just as the overlapping circles in Figure 1 indicate, we are already experiencing the glorious future of a new era. Green sprigs of life are already bursting from the ground. Dreamers are beginning to wake the nation. They are announcing the coming of a new order. Many individuals, churches, worshipers, and other dreamers are already laying hold of the future.

So, Here's the Deal!

Man is designed, created, redeemed and sustained by God. His whole life is a gift. He is, throughout his entire existence, dependent upon and indebted to his Creator. Therefore, his created posture is worship. The Westminster Catechism says it well: "Man's chief end is to glorify God and to enjoy Him forever."

Throughout all of human history, the creature—flawed though he is—has served as a creative instrument for expressing worship. Through music, vocation, literature and other expressions, the primal gratitude of the creature has groaned up out of his life and radiated out through waves of sight and sound. Imperfect, inadequate, croaking, dying, the sounds exhale from his corporeal existence and are offered up as the best the creature can jabber to his God.

How humanity offers up that worship changes from age to age. Inevitably and essentially, man's worship of his Creator is always uttered through the available paradigms, technologies, languages and even religions of the times.

This book will look at that evolution of worship throughout history as well as suggest what it is going to look like in the future. By examining the metamorphosis arising from technological advancement, evolving forms of communication and other patterns and media, we will gather around some available windows which offer a view of the future.

Glen Roachelle once said, "Sometimes we have to tolerate confusion and ambiguity while we wait for the contractions of history to give birth to a new era." While most people may not describe it that succinctly or eloquently, most are aware of a prevailing and bewildering sense of confusion and ambiguity. What they may not possess, however, is a sense of perspective about it: *these things are merely the beginning of birth pangs.*

The contractions are getting stronger and closer together. A new world is being born. Let's go explore it!

Notes

1. Jacques Ellul, *The Presence of the Kingdom* (Colorado Springs, CO: Helmers & Howard, 1989), p. 6.
2. Don Eberly, telephone interview by Ed Chinn, n.d.
3. Brian D. McLaren, *Reinventing Your Church* (Grand Rapids: Zondervan Publishing House, 1988), p. 80.
4. In this book, organic means "a living thing" as opposed to things artificial, imposed and/or contrary to nature. It also suggests the primal, original, natural, pristine character of created and living things.
5. *Webster's New World Dictionary* defines radical as "of or from the root or roots..." Webster's 1828 dictionary offered additional elucidations: "Primitive; original; underived....In botany, proceeding immediately from the root; as a radical leaf..."
6. Robert Putnam, "The Strange Disappearance of Civic America," *The American Prospect,* no. 24 (winter 1996), pp. 1-18.

CHAPTER THREE

I FEEL GOOD!

I found the exit and peeled off the freeway. Cars were already backed up. I looked at my watch; I was still a half hour early. *I still have time,* I shrugged. Twenty minutes later I pulled into my parking spot and started my considerable hike to the entrance of one of the fastest-growing churches in America. I was not at all sure I wanted to be there. But my friend had strongly recommended it. This contemporary psalmist had captured the sublime, worshipful majesty of the gathering by his solemn announcement, "The band is totally out there. They are kicking!"

As I entered the vast auditorium, the ushers were telling everyone to stay together so that each section would be filled up. Although there were four aisles, we all had to walk single file down the same one. I could not sit where I wanted. The other pews were roped off. It felt like a military maneuver. Soon the mechanized efficiency had dropped me into my designated seat. I sat looking around the "stall" at all the other "cattle." I was sitting with people I did not know; I was uncomfortable.

The choir and the worship team began to perform. The sound was good (but very loud). The choir robes were color coordinated, the band was in black, the platform lights were bright. The atmosphere was rockin' and hot. Four cameras on large platforms panned and arched in large circles, blocking the audience.

The architecture, the activities, and the technology all told me a perverse truth: This event was designed primarily for those who would watch it through television screens later. All the real live people filling the auditorium were only part of the production; we were props for the real audience—the "electronic audience." Of course, I also knew that the nonexistent electronic audience had more value to the church than those assembled in this great auditorium.

Is this what the Church has come to? I mumbled to myself. *The Tonight Show!*

WHAT IS WORSHIP?

> The Scotch catechism says that man's chief end is "to
> glorify God and enjoy Him forever." But...these are the
> same thing. Fully to enjoy is to glorify. In commanding
> us to glorify Him, God is inviting us to enjoy Him.[1]
> —C. S. Lewis

Perhaps no other arena of life symbolizes the decline of an era like worship.

Worship is the inevitable result of the creature catching a glimpse of eternal reality and responding. When mortals see—however fleeting or imperfect—a glimpse of the perfection and beauty of God's attributes, their spirit pushes up out of their earthbound carnality to declare—however feebly and inadequately—something about the reality they behold. Such profoundly transcendent suspensions represent the highest, noblest and *most purely enjoyable* moments of the creature's existence. They are passageways between earth and heaven. In those moments, worshipers are able to "slip the surly bonds of earth" and enter a dimension where they find pristine and total enjoyment of His presence.

That is the focal point of our created duality—our citizenship in earth and heaven.

THE HOMELESS WORSHIPERS

A Gallup survey reports that 38 percent of all church-going Americans are attending church less frequently than they did five years ago. In his research into why people are leaving the Church, William Hendrix wrote that one of the most-cited reasons for bailing out was that the Church was just "not worshipful. They did little to help people meet God."[2]

I and many of my friends are in the same place. For the past four years, our family has felt spiritually "homeless." Of course, we have a personal pastor who loves, cares and intercedes for us. But we're in that group that cannot find worship in any church setting. Like so many of my deeply committed, passionately devout friends, we have had it with superficial, human-centered services. We cannot take it anymore. The cry of many hearts today (including mine) is, Where is God? How can we meet Him?

We are experiencing a crisis of joy. We cannot find that "zone" where we behold the resplendent character of our Lord and from which inexplicable joy fills our hearts.

FORK IN THE ROAD

In 1994, the North American Summit on the Future of Worship convened 29 denominations in Nashville to discuss the future of worship. I was there with Robert Webber to represent some of the nondenominational churches and ministries. I was amazed that all the participants seemed to have the same concern: How can we renew our worship and be more relevant to our society? Yet the hardest thing for most of us was to be open to change. Almost everyone thought if we changed what "we do" it would compromise who "we are."

Most of us have made small steps in a direction that we thought would bring the best results: seeker meetings, contemporary versus traditional, Vineyard instead of gospel, or mixing praise and worship with more traditional hymns. We attend the latest conferences to get the latest tips and tools. But all these "baby steps" only connect with the externals which simply do not deal with the real issue. Many leaders are asking, Where do we go? Where do we turn? With so many choices and options available to leaders today it is easy to grasp the newest, the best and the most talked about. However, changing the external aspects of worship only changes the "image" of worship and not the "integrity" of worship. In the final analysis, all of this adds greater confusion and deepens the erosion of joy.

HOW DID WE GET HERE?

So, how did we get into this homeless crisis where Christians wander to find a substantive worship and fellowship? I believe it is just another feature of a dying era. It's probably another thing we have to tolerate while "the contractions of history give birth to a new era."

With the advent of an electronic age, more technologically sophisticated and "impressive" styles of worship flourished. Christians rushed in (sincerely, I believe) to utilize new technologies for enhancing their deep spiritual groanings of humanity to connect with the Creator. This desire sparked an explosion of new sounds of worship! However, that created a slippery slope for worship, too. Perhaps inevitably, worship slid into the realm of "experts"—worship leaders, planners, hired musicians, light technicians, audio-engineers, etc.

Of course, many churches did not, or could not, make such a "radical" change. However, rather than remaining (or moving into) genuine worship, they were washed into a crystallized, traditional backwater—unable to move into new sounds and unable to focus on the presence of God. Traditionalism was simply a reaction to something new. They were living in a new culture, but held to traditions that didn't fit that culture.

So, both groups lost the perspective that worship is a vertical reality. Both groups wandered into an illusion—that if they followed the "new formulas," they would "do worship."

Now the Church is all over the map in its efforts to find and worship God and serve the needs in the world. Week after week, Christians gather in a public place set apart for the worship of Christ. Believers congregate to celebrate, communicate, commemorate and participate and yet too many times they return home knowing that their purpose for gathering was not accomplished.

Too often the Church simply does not connect with its exalted Head—Christ. The presence of God was not encountered and the interaction with the Lord was shallow and rushed. The service is planned, sequenced, timed and flawlessly executed by the "experts." But the worship service remains flat, lifeless and dispiriting.

We live in an era that one leader has described as "the flowering of feelings." Over the past few decades, the subjective has surpassed the objective as the measurement of reality. Of course, that has influenced our walk with God. To a large degree, the Church has moved from faith to feelings. Commenting on Psalm 125, Eugene Peterson wrote:

> My feelings are important for many things....But they tell me next to nothing about God or my relation to God. My security comes from who God is, not from how I feel. Discipleship is a decision to live by what I know about God, not by what I *feel* about Him or myself or my neighbors. "As the mountains are round about Jerusalem, so the Lord is round about his people." The image that announces the dependable, unchanging, safe, secure existence of God's people comes from geology, not psychology.[3]

I FEEL, I FEEL,
I FEEL AND I FEEL
GOOD. IT'S
UNDERSTOOD...
FEELINGS ARE GOOD.

—NEUROTIC OUTSIDERS

When feelings become the purpose and goal of worship, emotional stimuli and external aids will be used to reach that goal. The result is the same kind of manipulation used in television, movies, music and video games. The worshiper who sought *feelings* ends up *feeling* used and abused and can even develop an addiction to the experience. Perhaps that is why some go home from church and say, *Something was wrong with the worship; I just didn't get the same feelings I normally get.*

Feelings are not of themselves bad in Christian worship for the

Lord says to worship Him with all our souls (see Luke 10:27). When our desire and intent are simply to attain good feelings, we lose the reality and purpose of worship. Our worship then becomes humanistic and is a mere by-product of electronic manipulation. Rather than touching and worshiping our God, it moves into spooky dimensions of mystical and sensual experience.

So here we are: We've cranked up the music, jumped and shouted, pushed all the feelings buttons and achieved 600 aerobic points. We're going for "I feel, I feel, I feel and I feel good, it's understood...feelings are good."

ILLUSIONS OF WORSHIP

Subsequent chapters will examine the markings of the emerging era. We will look at the future of worship. However, we have to face reality about the contemporary state of worship. Therefore, I have catalogued seven *illusions of worship* associated with the dying Church era.

1. WORSHIP IS A COMMODITY.

Tom Kraeuter reminds us, "Worship has become a commodity...we can become so interested in doing things 'right' to get the 'right' response from the people that we miss the whole point..."[4] Many times, in our work to have a "great service," we become so caught up in "doing" the service that we do not connect with God. The worship itself becomes the end—great music, mighty anthem, choir special, perfectly delivered sermon, and touching benediction.

Sally Morgenthaler adds:

> The fact is, great musical performances, thought-provoking drama, touching testimonies, relevant messages, and apologetics about God and faith are wonderful

tools God can use to touch the seeker's mind and heart. Notice, however, that their operation does not hinge on any sort of movement or response from those in attendance. They are all examples of presentation, and presentation does not require people to give anything of themselves back to God. It does involve the listener or observer in any of the expressions of worship: heartfelt praise, adoration, reverence, thanksgiving, repentance, confession, or commitment.[5]

It appears that most of the Church is more interested in the commodity of worship than in its true purpose; the look and sound of the product, how it's received, the "market research," and ratcheting the product to new features.

2. WORSHIP IS A QUEST FOR PLEASURE.

The music was cranked. Everyone was on their feet. The worship team was groovin'. Suddenly, women formed lines in the left and right aisles and began to dance in circles. They were smiling, clapping, and kicking up their feet. Skirts twirled higher and higher.

Devotion in motion is very biblical. There is a "time to dance." But what concerns me about "experience-oriented worship" is the attention given to the creature. When worshipers watch "devotion in motion" then they are not totally focused on the Creator and no worship occurs!

One of the results of our cultural subjectivity is that we have become addicted to sensory stimulation. An insatiable appetite for pleasure runs rampant in our society. This has certainly crept into and influenced worship. Of course, it's about time that we enjoyed our worship, but there is a pervasive assumption that pleasure is the goal. We now—even Christians—tend to focus on the carnal, temporal and pleasurable in a quest for fulfillment.

We've become pleasure seekers, lustfully pursuing what makes us feel better and stimulates our senses. Too often this is how we measure whether or not it was a "good service."

3. WORSHIP IS MUSIC.

Worship is not defined as music in the Bible. Not once. However, many Christians think worship is a synonym for music; most assume that musical ability is a prerequisite for worship. Therefore, nonmusical folks often believe they are excluded from participation. Worship then becomes more entrenched in the realm of the professionals.

The focus on the "excellence of worship," somewhat perpetuated by the "worship tape" phenomenon, has further distanced the "nonmusical" worshipers, thereby promoting platform-driven worship.

Today, worship is increasingly the territory of professional musicians—those hired to plan, practice, lead and "do" the worship. Sometimes the congregation gets the impression that you have to be as gifted in music and communication skills to be able to worship.

4. WORSHIP REQUIRES PROPS.

What would happen in your church if "the worship hour" approached and there were no hymnals, no video projector, no choir and no worship team? What if there were no one on the platform and nothing to look at?

Would you sit in silence because there were no "crutches"? Would you start talking about today's football game? Would you just go home? Or...would you focus on the Lord and press on into His presence anyway?

David worshiped the Lord all alone under the stars as he watched the sheep. Most of us have been gathered around a meal or a friend's hospital bed when the inclination of our hearts turned to spontaneous, unassisted worship. Those are splendid, cherished, longed-for moments of intimacy with our Lord. Worshipers experience those God encounters as *a way of life*. The immature and nonworshipers only worship in the confines of a service and would be lost without the props to carry them along and help them worship.

I've seen this happen in large congregations of believers also. Waylon Jennings is right: "Maybe it's time we get back to the basics of life." That includes worship that is rooted in a heart of gratitude and flows out in adoration regardless of what crutches or amplifiers are available.

5. WORSHIP IS A BIG DEAL.

Most churches in the United States, in fact 90 percent—have less than 100 people. One hundred thousand have fewer than 35 people in attendance. The worship "departments" of these churches are very small.

Incredibly, most of the contemporary "models" of worship do not work in 90 percent of the churches of America! These models often have a rhythm section, synthesizer, choir, vocal ensemble and a brass section. They are utilized, validated, and driven by worship conferences, megachurches and publishing companies. Something is wrong here. Where are the worship models that serve the smaller churches? I'm talking about the churches that do not have a rhythm section, PA system or video projector. Aunt Thelma plays the piano and John sometimes brings his guitar to this meeting of 35 worshipers. There is no platform, no ushers, no choir and no pews. This group meets in a home or a coffee shop.

Today, worship—simply because it is a big deal—is too often business driven rather than ministry or theology driven. The worship leaders tend to mimic their favorite worship artist and play the production numbers they heard on the greatest worship tape. Therefore, it is not surprising that many worship teams are sometimes nothing more than a frustrated garage band trying to play the latest hits.

6. WORSHIP IS RELEGATED.

According to Robert Webber, "The congregation is little more than an audience." However, he continues, "The focus of worship is not experience, not a lecture, not the music, not entertainment, but Jesus Christ—His life, death, and resurrection."[6] That, of course, is an intensely personal reality; it cannot be delegated to others.

Unfortunately, much of our worship is dominated by the worship leader or pastor. They are responsible for "doing," or producing, a good service while the rest of the flock of folks sit in neat rows staring at the head of the person in front of them participating in worship only when motivated by their feelings, moods, or the manipulations of the worship leader.

Sadly, the focus of most worship experiences is on the platform and the players of worship. An elite few control the worship. The rest are effectively groupies who gather to hear their favorite music group play the style of music they like and groove along, but do not become part of the center of worship.

This philosophy of leadership has persuaded (or manipulated) people to relinquish their priesthood to professionals. In this system of worship leadership, individual gifts only muddy up the water. I'm sure that this has been unintentional, but nevertheless the results are the same.

7. WORSHIP STYLES ARE UNALTERABLE.

A certain pastor was pleased that the use of a synthesizer in his church on Sunday morning had proven to be a wonderful complement and enhancement to the worship. He also felt the service had been enhanced by the sweet sounds from the "string" and the "angel breath" patches. However, on Monday the pastor was surprised by an urgent call from an irate caller. "What was that new sound that we heard during the worship Sunday? I don't think it should be used in the Church! It's the sound of the world."

The pastor weathered the stormy complaint. He recognized what the real issue was when the caller concluded by shouting, "We've never done that before!" This wasn't a worship issue at all—it was anger aroused by the fear and tension that comes from change.

The movie *Sister Act* is also a great parable about the dynamics of change.

The church in the movie was landlocked in an alien environment and disconnected from its purpose. It was focused on traditions and survival. Then change—in the form of Whoopi Goldberg as an "unchurched" lounge singer—walked in the door. The church didn't want, understand, like or value the agent of change. But through that agent, the church convulsed into a reconnection with its mission and moved into a new dimension of worship.

"New" is always a threat. And the older we get the harder it is to change (Wonder how I know that?). This is a human problem. Because the Church is an established (and predominantly conservative) institution, this mentality is particularly insidious.

SURVIVING IN THE NEUTRAL ZONE: *WORSHIP ANYWAY*

In his excellent book *Managing Transitions*, business consultant William Bridges identified the stages of change. He said the first stage is simply understanding that "transition begins with letting go of something." The second stage is entering the *neutral zone.* "This is the no-man's-land between the old reality and the new (see Figure 2). It's the limbo between the old sense of identity and the new. It is a time when the old way is gone and the new doesn't feel comfortable yet."[7]

Of course, the *neutral zone* is another way of expressing the overlap period between a dying era and an emerging one (Figure 2). I believe it is accurate to say we are living in the *worship neutral zone.* We are in the "no-man's-land between the old reality and the new." So what does that mean for worshipers? Are we to just go into spiritual hibernation?

I don't think so. I believe we should worship!

Eugene Peterson addressed the conduct of the worshiper in the neutral zone, "Feelings are great liars...Worship is an act which develops feelings for God, not a feeling expressed in an act of worship. When we obey the command to praise God in worship, our deep, essential need to be in relationship with God is nurtured."[8]

I believe we should come into God's presence with singing (see Ps. 100:2) and that we will often experience the charismata.

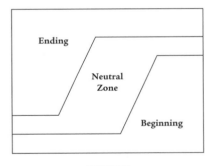

FIGURE 2

However, this *tradition* tends to make the worshiper dependent on an existential experience to substantiate his standing with God; if we don't "feel" God, we wonder if we are in right standing with Him. This is a feminine trait; it is a feelings orientation.

We must ask ourselves: Can we go to the assembly of believers and worship Him even if, say, we're in a "noncharismatic" environment? Can we lift up our hearts to Him even if the lights are not dimmed? Can we *command* our tired bodies to get out of bed and go join the throng of worshipers even when we don't feel like it?

Yet, what if the neutral zone lasts the rest of our lives? Does that mean that we will not move beyond the feminine, subjective, emotion-driven basis for declaring worship? That is why there is a great need for Christians to be fathered in the Lord. Only by being fathered can we grow up. Our paradigms and expectations of worship must grow up if we are to survive the neutral zone.

GROW UP IN ALL
ASPECTS INTO HIM,
WHO IS THE HEAD,
EVEN CHRIST.

—EPHESIANS 4:15

For example: We shouldn't think that God must speak continually. This certainly was not the case in the Old or New Testaments. There were long periods where God did not speak at all. The prophets were not full-time in ministry; they had a life. Yet we have a "TV episode" view of God's activity and voice; we expect dramatic and significant things every week. However, if God chose never to speak again in our lifetime, such silence should stir us to explore or obey all that He has already said to us! That's maturity—that's exercising victorious faith in the neutral zone—that's reclaiming home!

Let's act like mature worshipers and exercise victorious faith in the neutral zone. Let's come home.

Notes

1. C. S. Lewis, *Reflections on the Psalms* (New York: Harcourt, Brace, & World, 1958), pp. 96, 97.

2. William Hendrix, *Exit Interviews: Revealing Stories of Why People Are Leaving the Church* (Chicago, IL: Moody Press, 1993), p. 260.

3. Eugene Peterson, *A Long Obedience in the Same Direction* (Downers Grove, IL: InterVarsity Press, 1980), p. 83.

4. Tom Kraeuter, "Worship Is a Verb" *Psalmist* (Feb./March 1992), p. 25.

5. Sally Morgenthaler, *Worship Evangelism* (Grand Rapids, MI: Zondervan Publishing House, 1995), p. 48.

6. Robert Webber, *Worship Is a Verb* (Waco, TX: Word Books, 1985), p. 12.

7. William Bridges, *Managing Transitions* (Reading, MA: Addison-Wesley Publishing Company, 1991), p. 5.

8. Peterson, *A Long Obedience in the Same Direction,* p. 50.

CHAPTER FOUR

BIRTH OF A NEW ERA

Births are messy. A baby's arrival is anything but elegant; his or her advent is well lubricated with primordial slime and accentuated by screams. Future poets, priests and presidents all come sliding into life in the most graphically ignoble postures and circumstances. None of us would want our future value appraised at that moment!

Much of the chaos the world is experiencing is simply the birth of a new era. It is messy, undignified and even vulgar. We are witnessing the nascence of new ideas, attitudes, economies, technologies and structures. Some of them don't look like anything that could grow up to be clean and respectable; they are just a mess.

We are living through an historic and fundamental shift in the foundations of society. Everything is convulsing as we move into the third millennium (for some reason, millenniums always seem to be times of convulsion and metamorphosis). Radical change is

THE GLOBAL AGE THAT REPLACED THE INDUSTRIAL AGE SUBSCRIBED TO A DIFFERENT SET OF VALUES.
THE DIFFERENCE WAS EASY TO SEE BUT NOT EASY TO DEFINE.
IT WAS LIKE THE DIFFERENCE BETWEEN THE FACE OF A DYING OCTOGENARIAN AND THE FACE OF A NEWBORN BABY.

—GERALD CELENTE
TRENDS 2000[1]

shaking the cultural, financial, political, scientific, communications, and moral pillars upon which civilization rests. Consider this short list of a few global convulsions—some of history's contractions—in just the past ten years:

- Collapse of the Berlin Wall
- Disintegration of the Soviet Union
- Free elections in South Africa and the dismantling of apartheid
- Global increase of terrorism (Lockerbie, Oklahoma City, World Trade Center)
- Pro-democracy occupation of Tiananmen Square; government killings
- Pope John Paul II visits Cuba
- Public disgrace of high-profile ministries
- Global migration threatens to destabilize nations[2]
- DNA "fingerprinting" becomes admissible as evidence in criminal cases
- Development and expansion of the Internet
- Currency crashes
- Year 2000 computer problem (Y2K)
- Cloning of animals

All of these turning points contain simultaneous death and birth exchanges. They reflect the global metamorphosis captured in "the difference between the face of a dying octogenarian and the face of a newborn baby."

Management guru Peter Drucker says that "some time between 1965 and 1973 we passed over...a divide and entered 'the next century.' We passed out of creeds, commitments, and alignments that had shaped politics for a century or two. We are in political *terra incognita* with few familiar landmarks to guide us." He then describes one of the more significant markings of that transitional divide, "...salvation by society—the faith which since the eighteenth century's Enlightenment had been the dominant force and main engine of politics...is gone for good."[3]

Consider these startling realities which are related to the collapse of "salvation by society": For the first time, mankind is reaching a consensus that the best form of government is representative, multiparty democracy (21 of these changes have happened in Africa alone in a recent two-year period). Also, for the first time, the world is reaching agreement on the best form of economy: free markets. This is unprecedented; any country that does not comply will be trapped in the backwater of poverty.

However, although the world is moving closer to governmental and economic consensus, the *culture* of the world is still up for grabs. The main forces leading the way are humanism, New Age, Islam and Christianity. It is therefore necessary for our reference points—our paradigms—to change so we can navigate through this emerging new world.

For example, the culture of the United States has (over the past few decades) slowly changed from a Judeo-Christian-based society to more of a Roman-Greco democracy. Not only has

WHOLE LOTTA SHAKIN' GOIN' ON!

—JERRY LEE LEWIS

the Judeo-Christian "center" moved, but because of cultural digital-ization, there is no center at all—the center cannot be recaptured because it doesn't exist! Yet many evangelical Christians are still reacting (via numerous "center-recovery" efforts) to the loss of "market dominance" and the corresponding increase of pluralism. They are still trying to recapture, through politics, protest and debate, the Christian culture that once represented America.

FROM ROMANCE TO REALITY

Perhaps it is time to abandon the sentimental quest for "Christian restoration" and simply move out into the new pluralism with radical faith in the Creator and Owner of it all (maybe He's capable of taking care of His own stuff). The apostle Paul offers insight on how to do that.

> And Paul stood in the midst of the Areopagus and said, "Men of Athens, I observe that you are very religious in all respects. For while I was passing through and examining the objects of your worship, I also found an altar with this inscription, 'TO AN UNKNOWN GOD.' What therefore you worship in ignorance, this I proclaim to you" (Acts 17:22,23).

The apostle Paul's Areopagus speech represents model conduct for the Christian in a pluralistic society. He did not react to, nor attack, their paganism; he simply served them by revealing a new perspective toward something they already honored. He made their picture of the unknown clearer. He did not react to, nor tear down, their belief system; he expanded it. He didn't lock up over their cultural assumptions; he gave them a new paradigm for those assumptions.

Pauline scholar F. F. Bruce has commented on Paul's attitude by writing, "If men whom his hearers recognized as authorities had used language which could corroborate his argument, he would quote their words, giving them a biblical sense as he did so."[4]

I often wonder if I had been there at the Areopagus, would I have been able to get past my own romantic provincialism in order to even see the realities of Athenian culture? Would I have understood Paul's attitude? Would I have found myself in unfamiliar territory with an old map?

THE NEED FOR NEW MAPS OF REALITY

When we moved into our new home in Grapevine, Texas, a few years ago, we were the first ones in the new subdivision. It was wonderful to have all the space around us, and the view was great. However, we could not get the cable company to put in the lines for our television because we were not on their maps, and until we existed on a map they would not come out and service us. Incredibly, the back of our lot was the border of another subdivision that was on the cable company's map. A cable box was plainly visible just a few feet from our border! It was an easy fix, but they simply could not see it. Because we were not on their map, they thought we didn't exist. So, many of us went ahead and purchased satellite systems.

A few years later the cable company came knocking on our door trying to sell us their cable services. I asked, "Why didn't you come when we needed you? Sorry, but we satisfied our needs in other ways." Because the cable company's maps were not current, they simply could not see—and therefore missed their opportunity with—us.

Many bureaucratic and hierarchical systems, businesses and yes, churches have old maps of the new world. The world has changed, but because their maps have not changed, they do not see it. When maps are outdated, they are worthless in new terrain. Because of outdated maps, many Christians simply cannot see what Drucker calls "the new realities."

THE ISSACHARIAN CHALLENGE[5]

For some reason, there is often more reality within the world around us than within the Church. Could we (Christians) be so full of tradition and crystallized perspectives that we are like those who try to explore new territory with outdated maps? Although it sometimes seems to me that the Lord should be shaking His Church into reality, He doesn't. He just slowly changes everything around us and watches to see what we will do. Throughout history, those who considered themselves as "God's children" have often failed that test.

I remember Christians from another era confronted by change. They fought it by pounding pulpits (or car fenders or kitchen tables) and protesting, "But the Lord doesn't change!" Well, of course He doesn't. But, that isn't (and never was) the issue. In fact, cultures—wineskins—are always in a state of change. As the psalmist declared,

> All of them will wear out like a garment; Like clothing Thou wilt change them...But Thou art the same, and Thy years will not come to an end (Ps. 102:26,27).

When God folds up an age like a worn-out garment and puts it away, that always seems to force change on those of us who happen to hang out in the old epoch! And, that calls for us to understand the times. History carries special honor for people who understand such times. People like Simeon and Anna (see Luke 2), Frederick

Douglass, Abraham Lincoln and Winston Churchill are revered, at least in part, because they had an uncanny sense of the times in which they lived. Even contemporary figures like Bill Gates or Warren Buffett are admired because they seem to have an intuitive sense of the times.

WISDOM CRIES OUT IN THE MARKETPLACE

If you really want to understand the times, I would (sadly) have to direct you to the business section of the local bookstore, and not the Christian bookstores—*Wisdom cries out in the marketplace.*[6] Business is often a better source for wisdom and truth about the times than the Church is. One of the reasons for this: The world is hungry for truth and reality. People will read and ingest truth even if it doesn't fit their paradigms. Another reason is that the dollar forces businesses to be current with trends and realities. When you have an objective standard of measurement (like a financial bottom line), it is easier to hear the truth since there is a determination to capture wisdom and truth, in order to stay current, relevant, and profitable. Therefore, books like *7 Habits of Successful People, First Things First,* and *Principle Based Management* are flowing like rivers throughout the business world.

Something is missing, however, in the business world's approach to truth. For example, in the 1980s, a good source of marketplace wisdom was Tom Peters' *In Search of Excellence.*

THE SONS OF ISSACHAR, MEN WHO UNDERSTOOD THE TIMES, WITH KNOWLEDGE OF WHAT ISRAEL SHOULD DO.

—1 CHRONICLES 12:32

Although the driving concept of the book was excellence, it was basically a one-dimensional application of wisdom. It lacked one ingredient—spiritual depth and variegated context of eternal truth, integrity, and faith that would have caused it to "stick to the ribs." Understandably limited in purpose and audience, the book fell short of presenting where the truth of excellence comes from.

That missing ingredient—a spiritual foundation—calls for the Church to serve society in the same way Paul served the Athenians. Paul recognized that no one had captured truth for his audience better than Epimenides, Aratus or Plato. So, Paul utilized their words and provided a spiritual depth the Athenians lacked. The Greek perspective that there was an "unknown god" (see Acts 17:22-34) was an opportunity for Paul to use the cultural truth the Greeks had captured as a springboard into a deeper reality—spiritual understanding.

Perhaps it is time for the Church on the edge of a new millennium to just admit it doesn't have the same grasp on wisdom as the marketplace. After all, wisdom belongs to God; He can do whatever He chooses with it. If Stephen Covey or Bill Cosby or Marianne Williamson capture truth and wisdom better than the Church, let's recognize it, honor it, and then find how we can support the truth in our time.

GLIMPSES OF THE NEW ERA

"A new civilization is emerging....We face the deepest creative restructuring of all time."[7] These words of Alvin Toffler find their echo in the thoughts of Harvard's Harvey Cox: "We find evidence for a new phase of history in virtually every field of human endeavor."[8] "New phases of history" are trying to form in the Church as well. Church growth specialist Charles Arn sees a new paradigm which will reinterpret the world.[9] Futurist scholar

Rex Miller envisions a new medium that will redefine society and change the way we worship, and Canadian theologian David Lochhead perceives a new awareness that will revise reality.[10]

Although we see through a glass darkly, many believe we're entering a future where we will see life less rationally and more intuitively, less analytically and more holistically, less literally and more metaphorically. In short, we're shifting from an intellectual religion to a personal spirituality, from a God of philosophy to a God of prophecy, from a God of apologetics to a God of apocalypse. Indeed, historian William Irwin Thompson calls our time "a spiritual evolution." He says it is actually creating the new technologies of a digital age...it is actually midwifing the birth of a new humanity.[11] In other words, maybe technology is not birthing a new spirit; perhaps the Spirit is birthing a new technology!

AND THE WORD OF THE LORD CAME TO ME SAYING, "WHAT DO YOU SEE, JEREMIAH?"

—JEREMIAH 1:11

Something new and possibly transcendent is blowing in fields like physics, biology and astronomy. Increasingly, artists are witnessing a future far different from the materialism of the industrial age. Increasingly, spiritual awareness is reaching critical mass in the gravity pull of a new millennium.

According to marketing legend, when Pepsi introduced its soft drink into Taiwan, the world famous "Come alive with Pepsi" actually translated into Taiwanese: "Pepsi will bring your ancestors back from the dead." As we enter the new territory of the future, do we understand the words and images, do we perceive the light and sound waves of that new era?

A new world is being born. That new world, however messy, undignified and vulgar, is not the issue—our relationship to it is. How we relate to this new era is largely determined by what we see. Numerous times the Bible reveals God asking His servants, "What do you see?" Jonah failed in his mission because he simply could not see Nineveh; he saw a messy, undignified, vulgar, even barbaric city. But God saw a "great city"! (see Jon. 1:2; 4:11). Just because we have perception does not mean we see accurately.

FIGURE 3

One of the most famous optical illusions of all time illustrates this very well (Figure 3). There are two women in the picture. Which one do you see? The relationship of an individual, a church, or any other unit to an era or sovereign move of God faces the same dilemma. Does it see an old and decrepit creature or a young and radiant beauty?

History can be understood as a record of how people view reality. Sadly, "God's people" seem to have fared no better than the heathen in their view of, and response to, truth in their time.

What about those of us who now stand in another historical overlap of two ages? Can we only see the one in decline? Or will we catch a glimpse of the future? Will our view be any more accurate than Jonah's?

Let me once again remind you that our chief purpose in life is to offer—through a myriad of expressions—worship of our Designer, Creator, Redeemer and Sustainer. And that worship will always be groaned through the paradigms, cultures, religions and other truth translators of our times.

Consider the following metamorphoses of worship, and man's response to them, throughout history:

- Development of Davidic worship in 2000 B.C.
- The Incarnation of the Word
- The death and resurrection of Christ
- The coming of the Holy Spirit (Upper Room)
- Persecution of A.D. 250-261 (martyrs and confessors)
- Constantinian worship reform
- Martin Luther's reform (A.D. 1512)
- Translation of the Bible from Greek to German
- Great Awakenings (1802-1867)
- The Pentecostal revival of 1901 in Los Angeles, California, and Topeka, Kansas
- Latter rain visitation in Saskatchewan and in the U.S. (1940s)
- Charismatic movement (1960-70s)
- Argentina Revival (1985)
- Convergence Movement (1990)
- Toronto and Pensacola Revivals (1995)

Each of these events and movements represented a monumental paradigm shift which created a whole new culture of worship. Many people—worshipers—missed the hour of visitation.

In case you've been living in a cave for a couple of decades, let me be the first to welcome you to the future! Once again, we are facing a new world. It will demand a paradigm shift if we are to perceive God's purpose and understand the hour.

THE TIMES THEY ARE A-CHANGIN'.

—BOB DYLAN

Change is here. There is no place to hide. It has *your* number and it takes no prisoners. It is bringing chaos and few of us are ready. Change challenges all the sacred assumptions of any set of traditions. It provokes religious reactions and drives tumult and chaos. We're facing the kind of historic change that lays some things in the grave while midwifing the birth of other things.

Earlier upheavals plodded along with agonizingly slow, blood-drenched dramas of war, revolt, famine or other calamities. Today, the times are shorter. The stakes are higher, the dangers greater.

THE FUTURE'S SO
BRIGHT, I GOTTA
WEAR SHADES.

—TIMBUK 3

Some look at the future through the eyes of hope. They seem to be in denial that the future could bring anything other than a fulfillment of their personal desires and comfort zones. They fail to recognize that change is God's broom. It sweeps worn-out ideas, attitudes and objectives away. No corner is spared.

Others view the future through fear. They see beyond the garden-variety demons to identify major principalities and powers hiding in the confusion. They see the "mother of all spiritual wars" sneering back at us amid the chaos. To them the status quo is sacred and is to be guarded and maintained at all cost. Because they are threatened, they think God is also threatened; they deduce He is asking them to make "holy war" on change. Of course, the more delusional adherents of this future view end up sitting in corners of padded rooms.

However, is there a third perspective, a worldview that is beyond hope and fear?

Yes, there is painful and cataclysmic upheaval. Doubtless we are witnessing a convergence of crises that seems unmatched in history—a coarsening culture, the devaluation of character, family deconstruction, health care inadequacy, imploding morality, urban decay, the uncertainties imposed by an increasingly global economy, and the loss of virtue in our leaders and institutions are just a few of the systems in crisis. All of our most promising solutions seem to only make conditions worse.

Nevertheless, can we look at the future—including the most fear-inducing factors—through the eyes of faith? Admittedly, we do not see the future accurately. But there is One who has never been afraid of the future. He is already there. He invites us to join Him.

Notes

1. Gerald Celente, *Trends 2000* (New York: Warner Books, 1997), p. 192.
2. "Migration is a greater threat to global stability than has been recognized. The sheer press of numbers of the very poor...is likely to become a steadily more destructive political force for Western democracies." Jessica Matthews, Senior Fellow at the Council on Foreign Relations as quoted in *Poughkeepsie* [NY] *Journal*, March 13, 1995.
3. Peter Drucker, *The New Realities* (New York: Harper & Row Publishers, 1989), pp. 3-11.
4. F. F. Bruce, *Paul: Apostle of the Heart Set Free* (Grand Rapids, MI: Eerdmans Publishing Company, 1977), p. 242.
5. Thanks to Glen Roachelle for this phrase.
6. See Proverbs 1:20. Note: I would distinguish between "natural" wisdom and divine revelation (the "hidden mysteries" of Ephesians 3:9). The marketplace seems to have a greater degree of natural wisdom. However, the Ephesians 3:10 referenced "wisdom of God" is to be made manifest *through the Church.*
7. Alvin and Heidi Toffler, *Creating a New Civilization: The Politics of the Third Wave* (Atlanta: Turner Publishing, 1995), pp. 12, 21.
8. Harvey Cox, *Fire from Heaven: The Rise of Pentecostal Spirituality and the Reshaping of Religion in the Twenty-first Century* (Reading, MA: Addison-Wesley Publishing Company, 1995), p. 301.

9. Charles Arn, "Are Your Paradigms Working for You or Against You?" *Ministry Advantage*, vol. 6, no. 4, Fuller Theological Seminary (July/Aug. 1996), p. 9.

10. David Lochhead, *Theology in a Digital World* (Etobicoke, Canada: United Church Publishing House, 1988), p. 28.

11. William Irwin Thompson, *Coming Into Being* (New York: St. Martin's Press, 1996), p. ix.

CHAPTER FIVE

CONSTANTINE: ENDINGS AND BEGINNINGS

The first Christian believers met in homes. Any assembly of the Church was an intimate, informal and joyful gathering. It usually featured a meal and was designed for total inclusion and participation. Every member was a vital and cherished part of the whole experience of worship. Paul described it well:

> When you assemble, each one has a psalm, has a teaching, has a revelation, has a tongue, has an interpretation. Let all things be done for edification (1 Cor. 14:26).

The environment in which the Church flourished for three centuries was a hostile one. "The testimony" was the primary mission of the Church. Each member was a crucial and responsible witness of the love of God according to His revelation of Christ. They all understood that they had authority to proclaim the gospel, heal the sick and cast out demons. Persecution was common. One's personal survival and comfort were not the issue; each disciple was a carrier, infected by and highly contagious with the gospel message and power. They may die a martyr's death tomorrow, but they were consumed by the mission. This mission was immediate, urgent, and not of this world. All believers participated; the world was their field.

When Roman emperor Constantine converted to Christianity in A.D. 312, the persecution of Christians ended. This was a pivotal moment in history because

> ...the accession of Constantine was the admission of the world that the life of Christ in His people is indestructible. The fires of persecution could not quench it, nor the floods of oppression overwhelm it. The enormous capacity of the spiritual life of the church to survive and to triumph over all the carnal means of the world hurled against it, stood as an unassailable fact...it was a triumph of the cross, the weakness and foolishness of God overcoming the strength and wisdom of men. The church had won. The great Roman Empire had to bow its head in defeat.[1]

But the plot thickens.

Constantine was also a statesman faced with formidable problems.

> The empire he had inherited was coming apart at the seams. He had sleepless nights about this fact. How could he conquer this problem? How bind the sprawling domains together again? How regain the ancient stability and inner cohesion? Then came the much celebrated "vision," a cross in the clouds, and the words "in hoc signo vinces" (in this sign conquer). There he had it!

Make the religion of Jesus the religion of the empire and then look to it to achieve the consensus that he, sacralist that he was, and remained, felt he had to have.[2]

Tragically, the Church became inverted in its mission and philosophy. The once persecuted minority—"called out ones"—became the "called in ones." Christians were called into the empire, the system, and into a structured Church. While it certainly had an appeal (no one really wants to be burned at the stake!), it also had a corrupting and denaturing effect on the radical nature of the Body of Christ. The Church, the world and the Roman Empire tuned out to be one and the same. To be a witness no longer presupposed a willingness to die for Christ in martyrdom, but to merely take the Church to the new territories conquered by the empire. The mission was now to convert the barbarians and pagans to the Christian culture and civilization. This radically altered the understanding of the Church. An encrustation of cultural "add-ons" began and Christianity was no longer as organic and simple as its pristine beginnings. The traditions of men, politics and organized institutions formed a "new" Christianity.

So, when did these add-ons get purged? They didn't. That's the problem. They've adapted, morphed and calved. However, we have the same encrustation problem. Today, seventeen hundred years later, regardless of all the revolutions of communication which we will examine in part II, we are still affected by the shift that began the erosion of full participation in the mystery.

WE JUST WANT TO WATCH

By A.D. 400, the Church had been profoundly affected by a new position of power afforded by the emperors Constantine and Theodosius. Constantine helped establish the Edict of Milan in

A.D. 313—official acceptance of Christians in the empire; Theodosius chose to merge Christianity with the Roman state religion in A.D. 380.[3] These milestones had two definite effects.

First, 87 years after the Edict of Milan the Roman Empire had gone from being less than 3 percent to 80 percent Christian—with no conversions! Second, the tax funds which had previously supported pagan religions now flowed exclusively to the Christian church. Consequently, some historians believe, pagan priests switched "companies." Even government officials and politicians became Christian priests because it was lucrative to do so.

The mission of the Church, once the province of "believers," was now the territory of elite religious leaders and the state! The clergy managed the religious rites and mysteries; they were the guardians of the sacred—the holy dispensers of the ministry of the Word. They decided what was truth, what was from God. They dispensed the sacraments, taught the faith, evangelized, and received the prophetic word.

After Constantine, the "laity" provided support for the institutionalized churches and a new clerical class. Their primary function was reduced to serving on committees, contributing to the finances and facilities so that the clergy could fulfill "their ministry."

> Many medieval churches were owned privately by wealthy laymen, monasteries, or bishops. The owner sold or passed on the property as he wished, and its revenues went into his pocket. He appointed the priest, had him ordained, and paid him. Many owners gave the parish to a priest as a "living," who as "rector," received all or most of the revenues...During some periods, church offices were bought and sold openly, and church officials lived sumptuously—"loaded with gold and clad in

purple," as one critic put it...The corruption so angered
people, they sometimes ransacked monasteries of killed
bishops.[4]

By the 1200s, almost all Christians had a pastor as a result of
the geographically defined parishes in which they lived. The clergy
served as agents for cultural consensus in their communities;
they presided over public ceremonies and the forgiving of sins. In
an exaggeration of this pattern, they became the mediators and
dispensers of a religion to the masses. The power and purpose of
the apostolic Church was lost.

WINDOWS TO HEAVEN: THE ARRIVAL OF ICONS

Christians in the Middle Ages may have been relatively illiter-
ate, but they were not ignorant of the Bible. The Bible played
an important role in the faith of every believer. It wasn't the
"printed" Word, but the "visual" Word that imparted truth and
strengthened them; mosaics, paintings, dramas, stained glass,
sculptures and icons became illuminated Bible stories and
characters.

Drama was a vital means of communicating Bible events
in the oral culture. Primary dramatic vehicles for the story
were mystery, morality and miracle plays with complete stage
sets, realistic props and talented actors. Even architecture
reflected the story; biblical scenes were carved in the stone of
buildings.

Icons were considered a ministry to the heart as well as to
the eyes. They were visual aids, helping the believer to recall
important biblical and Church events. It was believed, particularly in the Orthodox church, that the icons helped worshipers
visualize the invisible; they did not view them as idolatry. The
intent was to draw the worshiper's attention to the spiritual

realities above and beyond that icon. In the Middle Ages they were considered "windows to heaven."

THE INVENTION OF CHURCH BUILDINGS

When Constantine founded the city of Constantinople (Istanbul), he commissioned the building of pagan temples; some he designated as buildings for Christian meetings. Christians had met for almost three centuries in homes. Yet with the new temples, they began to meet in a "church building."[5] Constantine built these assembly buildings for Christians in Rome, Jerusalem and parts of Italy between A.D. 323 and 327. A church-building fad began all over the Roman Empire. Each building was given a name just as the pagan temples each had names. According to James Rutz, "We were headed straight for a totally different kind of Christian worship in a wholly different atmosphere from what the first century believer had ever dreamed of."[6] This began to displace traditional meetings in catacombs, synagogues, forest glens and the casual meetings in homes. The Church had made a turn: from being an interactive family to becoming an audience of "watchers."

Christians didn't even have an understanding about how to behave in a "church building." It was simply not "in the genes" of their spiritual heritage. For example, they tried to figure out whether they should sit on the floor or stand like in the pagan temples across the street. There were no chairs or pews. This caused a great debate and a marked difference between the Eastern and Western Church (the Italians dragged in benches and got comfortable and the Greeks stood...the Italian churches grew faster!).

SEPARATION OF CHURCH AND PEOPLE

People came pouring *en masse* into churches. As an "event management" reality, the pattern of the church services had to change to accommodate them. Ritual and structure became more important. Real Church leaders were few in number because of the great Christian persecution and execution under Diocletian (A.D. 303). So, some folks had to be drafted for leadership; the term "clergy" was introduced (it was what a pagan priest was called). They began to wear costumes to set themselves apart from the average Christian.

Eventually, the bishop and the clergy were seated separately from the congregation. In turn, less ranking ministers, singers and readers were placed behind them. Worship was removed from the people and became a function of the privileged. The bishop's seat (which earlier had been among the people) was now located behind the altar. Inevitably, it became a seat of power and honor and eventually a throne. Separated from the people and other clergy, the center of worship was no longer among the people, but upon the bishop and the clergy. The bishop slowly became an authority outside of the body of believers and lost the status of a servant within the Body of Christ.

Other changes further isolated worshipers from the presence of God:

- The language of worship was changed to Latin. Thereby, the role of the believer was even further diminished. They were reduced to watching the drama of worship played out in front of them.
- With rare exceptions, the Eucharist was received only by the clergy. This made the most sacred act of worship more remote, feared, and inaccessible.
- When the emperor became a fellow worshiper, Christians began to dress up. It was just not fitting to wear work clothes while participating in an event with

an emperor. We continued to "wear church clothes" for seventeen centuries!

THE CRYSTALLIZATION OF THE MYSTERY

Just as a photograph never depicts the present, but always the past, church structure always "manages" the *residue* of the mystery—the mystical presence of God in worship.

In *The Problem of Wineskins*, Howard Snyder articulated a vital truth: "Every age knows the temptation to forget that the gospel is ever new. We try to contain the new wine of the gospel in old wineskins—outmoded traditions, obsolete philosophies, creaking institutions, old habits. But with time the old wineskins begin to bind the gospel. Then they must burst, and the power of the gospel pours out once again. Many times this has happened in the history of the Church. Human nature wants to conserve, but the divine nature is to renew."[7]

So, the Constantinian era (when Christianity became an accepted belief by the state) created the same problem that people have in every other age of the Church—the filtering out of the potency of God's presence in worship through confining liturgical practices. Of course, no one means to gut the mystery. It just seems to be an inevitable, albeit unintended, result (and cycle) of the interaction between the throbbing reality of heaven and the carnality of man.

Here's how the problem develops: Something in our makeup insists that we make sense of life. We demand rules and guardrails that will make society governable and peaceful; we want to see God write words on rocks and hurl them into every public and private domain in the land, making the rules and boundaries clear for everyone ("Well, I guess *that* settles *that!*"). When God doesn't do that, we will do it for Him. We live with an assumption that order can be defined and imposed *through organ-*

ization. However, God rules an invisible kingdom that is difficult to quantify, control or define under our conventional thinking.

For example, Orthodox priests in the fourth century would dress in vestments reminiscent of Christ's royalty and spread incense above and around the worshipers signifying the presence of Jesus among His faithful. The incense would also represent the invisible presence of the Holy Spirit. "It was the intention of the Orthodox that all these various elements of worship help the members participate in worship with the totality of their personalities, and not just intellectually. The Orthodox believe that beauty—whether expressed in the colors and styles of icons, or through the beautiful vestments of the priests, or in the aromatic scents of incense—calls all the person's components to prayer."[8] It was designed to recall the heart-pounding, life-changing, mysterious reality of His presence.

The primary role for the worshiper became to look and listen—*there was still something to watch.* However, even when the meaning and purpose of the symbols and actions turned into dung, like fine sand sifting in and over time transforming a living tree through petrification, tradition and ritual "petrified" the sacred and holy realities of the mystery. It had all the gnarled beauty and texture of the once-alive tree, but it was cold stone.

DÉJÀ VU

Charles Simpson recently noted:

> By the fourth century, Christianity was codified and institutionalized...The once "Persecuted Church" became the "Persecuting Church." The Church that once proclaimed Christ's Kingdom, began to believe it *was* the Kingdom. The reign of Christ became the reign of clergy.[9]

It is easy, as armchair historians, to trivialize the issues and atmosphere which led to Constantianism. With a little work, one can imagine the stage on which Constantine sanctioned the Church. A thousand years after Constantine, Theodore Beza wrote, "After God had launched Christianity by unarmed apostles, He afterward raised up kings by whose wisdom He intended to protect His church..."[10] One can almost hear the "amens" and prophetic words and new worship choruses which affirmed the end of persecution and the "awakening of the Church." People in Constantine's time undoubtedly saw the Church's new visibility and militancy as the Lord's destiny for a "victorious Church."

Because of Constantine, many Christian mothers did not have to bury their sons. They probably went to meetings and said things like, "God is faithful. God is good. I just praise Him for His protection of my family." However, also because of Constantine, the Cross became a battle shield, Christians moved from being doers to watchers, and "church" became a place instead of the Body.

The Church is always—in every age and culture—vulnerable to seduction by the world systems. There are always compelling motivations for compromise. The Church in any age or culture, according to Ellul, "ought to find its own way, given it by God, which it alone can follow. It is only on this condition that the Church will cease to be a sociological movement, and be present in the world with the effectiveness given by the Holy Spirit." Ellul further points out:

> The enemies of the Church seek to turn it aside from its own way, in order to make it follow their way; the moment it yields it becomes the plaything of the forces of the world...From the human point of view this way of the Church in the world is foolish, utopian, and ineffective,

and we are seized with discouragement when we see what we really have to do in this real world.[11]

So, here we are in the Yogi Berra syndrome—it's *déjà vu* all over again! As in previous centuries, humanity has clumsily manhandled the eternal. The pulsating essence of the mystery has been lost. The Spirit has been grieved by our efforts to control it. Christians have become spectators. The Church has become hostile (downright dangerous!) to sinners who often believe the Kingdom and the Church are synonymous.

However, as in the fourth century with Constantine and in the centuries to follow, the generosity of God is breaking through the concrete of our carnality. He is transcending our best efforts. Even as we live in the decadence and death of a fading era, a new world is struggling through the birth canal.

WATER HOSES AND THUNDERSTORMS

The garden was parched and dying. The small boy directed a pitiful stream of water from a half-inch water hose onto the sun-cracked soil around the tomato plants, cucumber vines, carrot shoots, and corn stalks. The kid was tired and soaked with sweat.

Suddenly, he noticed a breeze. The shriveled tomatoes began to dance at the end of their blanched green branches. The dried-out corn stalks began to rattle. He heard the rumble of thunder; he turned to the west and saw the sky was already growing black! Then, he heard a voice. His father was running toward him from the barn, waving his arms and shouting, "Head for the house, son! It's coming! It's not going to miss us this time!"

The boy dropped the water hose and ran for the back door. As it slammed shut behind him, the sky split open. Water fell like it was being poured out of buckets. God had surely tipped the water jars of heaven (see Job 38:37). Then, from the back door, the little boy noticed something laying on the ground in the garden; the half-inch water hose was still spurting its meager stream.

History is like that. About the time that man exhausts his strength and best efforts to keep things alive, the grace and generosity of God shows up. It doesn't condemn water hoses; it just transcends and surpasses them. It speaks of resource and grace from "Him who is able to do immeasurably more than all we ask or imagine" (see Eph. 3:20, *NIV*).

Notes

1. John Kennedy, *The Torch of the Testimony* (Goleta, CA: Christian Books, 1965), p. 86.
2. Leonard Verduin, *The Reformers and Their Stepchildren* (Grand Rapids, MI: Eerdmans Publishing Company, 1964), p. 31.
3. James Rutz, *The Open Church: How to Bring Back the Exciting Life of the First Century Church* (Auburn, ME, SeedSowers, 1992), p. 48.
4. *Christian History,* vol. 15, no. 1 (1996), p. 2.
5. Rutz, *The Open Church,* pp. 46, 47.
6. Ibid., p. 47.
7. Howard Snyder, *The Problem of Wineskins* (Downers Grove, IL: InterVarsity Press, 1975), p. 16.
8. Alexander Melnyk, "What is Eastern Orthodoxy Anyway?" *Christian History,* vol. 7, no. 2, issue 18, (1988), p. 24.
9. Charles Simpson, "One Person at a Time," *One-to-One* (autumn, 1998), p. 7.
10. Verduin, *The Reformers and Their Stepchildren,* p. 83.
11. Jacques Ellul, *The Presence of the Kingdom* (Colorado Springs, CO: Helmers & Howard, 1989), p. 126.

PART II

ECHOES INTO THE FUTURE

Time is an invention, a human idea which gives (at the least the illusion of) some control and structure over life.

Dr. Yitzhak Hayutman of the Academy of Jerusalem has written that "time" came about because of an "awareness of death—of one's personal death and the possibility of the death of one's reference group, the tribe, the culture or even all humankind." Many today are understandably obsessed by the future because it seems to be moving in like a tidal wave. Moreover, it carries the possibility of death—personal, tribal, cultural and global. Therefore, many are immobilized by fear or confusion.

Perhaps the only way for the Church to prepare for such a tidal wave of change is to carefully listen to its past. The echoes of past worship and faith reverberate with truth through the present and into our future. In order to successfully navigate what lies ahead, we must come to understand the importance of how and why a communication medium shapes the perceptions and identity of the Church. This is not to suggest the Church retreat into traditionalism; rather, it is to encourage Christians to slip out of a "time-lock" and embrace a more eternal view of life— a view that might return us to the simplicity that characterizes Christ's attitude and message.

Over the last few years at The International Worship Leaders Institute, futurist and strategic planner Rex Miller has presented models, perspectives, and insights about the communication mediums that impact Church worship and organizational structure. The foundation and perspectives articulated in the following chapters are rooted in his tremendous research efforts. I am deeply indebted to his analysis and profound wisdom that explores the historical development and metamorphosis of communication mediums and their impact on faith and worship. The heart of this book would not have been possible without his keen articulation of future trends.

Miller's work is primary to understanding how a communication medium (the sensory conduit by which we see and process events around us) *shapes who we are,* how we view the world, and our fundamental concepts about faith and worship. Understanding the advantages and disadvantages of such powerful communication mediums offers Christians a light into how to best convey the gospel message to the world of today and tomorrow.

Our examination will begin with the oral tradition—the dominant medium of communication rooted in the Early Church. We will then turn to the printed word that flourished under the Protestant Reformation, followed by the advent of radio and television—electronic communication—that ushered in a new age for mass evangelism and teaching. Each of these communication delivery systems—spoken, printed, or electronic word—brought a new way of seeing and a new way of living with perceived truth.

These communication forms are now being overshadowed by the coming digital age. Our final examination (and the most provocative) will be focused on this new form of communication that is sweeping the world and how it is reshaping our understanding of the Christian community. The only way to grasp these changes is to know our past. If we are astute in listening to the ringing echoes of past worship and faith, we will discover a richer experience in His presence and a fresh way to share the power of the gospel to the world.

I AM GOD, AND THERE IS NO ONE LIKE ME, DECLARING THE END FROM THE BEGINNING.

—Isaiah 46:9.10

CHAPTER SIX

THE SPOKEN WORD

Elie Wiesel remembers the German invasion of his native Hungary in March 1944. He was 16 when he was torn from his traditional and loving Jewish family and pulled into the brutal teeth of Auschwitz and Buchenwald. Wiesel says "Everything changed overnight. A few words uttered by a man in uniform, and the order of Creation collapsed. Everything was dismantled; ties were severed, words were emptied of their meaning."[1]

"'Stay together,' my mother said. For another minute we did, clinging to one another's arms. Nothing in the world could separate us. The entire German army could not take my little sister from me. Then a curt order was issued—men on one side, women on the other—and that was that. A single order, and we were separated... What remains of that night like no other is an irremediable sense of loss, of parting. My mother and my little sister left, and I never said goodbye."[2]

He never saw them again. For a time, he and his father were together in a concentration camp. In one of the most moving segments of the book, Wiesel remembers his father's death.

> My father was getting worse. He was dying. It was the darkest day of my life...He shuddered and called my name. I tried to get up, tried to crawl to him, but the torturers were there, forbidding all movement. I wanted to cry out, "Hold on, Father, hold on. In a minute, a second, I'll be at your side. I'll listen to you, talk to you, I won't let you die alone." My father was dying and I was bursting with pain. I didn't want to leave him. But I did. I was forced to. They were beating me, I was losing consciousness. He moaned, and I waited for the torturers to go away. He was weeping softly, like a child, and I felt my chest coming apart.[3]

Although Nobel Prize winner Wiesel is known primarily as a writer, for many years he did not write a word about the loss of his family or any other holocaust experience. In his long-awaited memoir, he explains why: "The spoken word and the written word do not reflect the same experience...Rabbi Itzhak Lurie set nothing down on paper...Rabbi Nahman ordered that his writings be burned. The Zohar speaks of *galut hadibur*, the exile of the word...a chasm opens between them and their content; they no longer contain the meanings they once harbored."[4]

THE ORAL TRADITION

From the beginning of time until about five hundred years ago, the voice was the primary means of communication. In this oral tradition, there was no journal or electronic gizmo to collect and retrieve detailed history and everyday events. The collective memory of the community elders, storytellers and musicians recalled the past. In such a society, history was preserved and passed on as if it were occurring in the present; it came alive through ceremonial rituals and festivals. In his book, *Presence of the Word*, Walter Ong said, "primitive life is simultaneous in that it has no records, so that its conscious contact with its past is governed by what people talk about."[5]

Of all communication media, the oral tradition remains the most personal and powerful. But—although we still talk to one another—we have no idea what the oral tradition was about. This medium gave birth to Christianity and transformed the Western World. Yet today, our Greek-rhetoric words, our hollow dictionary definitions and our shallow television images survive as trivial cousins to their ancient ancestors.

For example, the oral tradition of the ancient Hebrews was—in the beginning—an *inspired* word, a prophetic word. Unlike modern words—known only by the brain—Hebrew "words" emerged first from the body. For Hebrew flesh uttered a depth of meaning that we are not capable of comprehending. They captured metaphorical sensations and endless somatic shades. Their bodies talked! These were viscerally communicated realities that spoke more from the intuitive heart than from the logical mind. The Hebrews boldly shared these truths with others through story, song, image, dance and drama.

In oral communication, face-to-face encounters are intimate and personal. The personal relationship is vital to the interactive communication process. The ear is the receptor. It is sensitive to volume, pitch, pacing and inflection and, therefore, creates a sense of inclusion and immediacy.

THE POWER OF THE SPOKEN WORD

People in oral cultures lived in tribes and villages. Most everyone knew all the others and their varying levels of relationships. Every person played a role and had a purpose. The bond of the community was strong. In such a society, commitments were to the family and to the larger "village family." There were few outside influences. The elders were the fountains of information and wisdom, the sources of history and identity. Therefore, one would not even consider breaking his ties with the elders. Their spoken words were the point of connection to personal and communal meaning.

In the oral society, understanding and truth were intimately connected with the speaker. One would sit at the feet of "the wise ones" to hear wisdom and understanding. Truth and revelation was an encounter with a person. Holy men, elders, witch doctors and priests, among others, carried the past and the future of the community. It is not coincidental that parents were respected and the fathers were honored.

The way of thinking and reasoning was dialectic. In other words, life was examined through analytical questions and answers. It was an interactive, relationship-based process of presenting a thesis, which generated its own opposite (antithesis), which would—through the vitality of the personal relationship—lead to synthesis. It is only an empty dialectic shell we observe today in the form of television programs like "Crossfire," on talk radio, and through other debate formats. Spoken words scream through the air like bullets. The speakers have no personal relationship. Therefore, they are incapable of arriving at synthesis.

Words, as they were used and respected in the oral tradition, were prophetic; prophecy was metaphoric and metaphors were artistic. In fact, in such a society, art, metaphor and prophecy were all essential synonyms of communication. Unlike today, words were used with great care and intent. *Believing* and *speaking,* for example, were identical. As imitators of their heavenly Father, the early Hebrews spoke "of nonexistent things...as if they existed" and "declaring the end and the result from the beginning" (Rom. 4:17; Isa. 46:10, *AMP.*). It's no surprise that in the middle of a drought, Elijah announced, "There is the sound of abundance of rain" (1 Kings 18:41, *AMP.*). Nor was it unusual when Jesus declared, "I have overcome the world" (John 16:33, *AMP.*), when—in reality—His victory became fact when He later died and rose again.

Oral words had power—not the power of the heroic ego, but a spiritual power greater than the speaker. And the speaker fully expected something awesome to happen. Each moment was charged with raw reality, immediate possibility, and manifest presence. The Hebrews knew that the *Word* of God and the *Spirit* of God were the same thing. And they knew from experience that the word they spoke went out and did some very heavy lifting! It moved with raw creative power, fulfilled its own prophecy, and manifested its own meaning. Unlike today's words which "supervene" in life—that is, they only add to—their words *intervened* in life—they actually changed life.

Spoken words incarnated power. We find these oral "words" in the sounds of the trumpets that flattened the walls of Jericho. We find them in the music of David's lyre that drove an evil spirit from Saul. We find them in the voices of the prophetic singers that led Judah's army while God defeated their foes. Carl Hausman sees that such spoken words "are active forces in the world," that they have the power to bring "something into being."[6] And Paul Ricoeur says metaphors have "the power not only to generate meaning but ultimately to change the world."[7]

In other words, prophetic metaphors can still empower today!

THE BASIS OF TRUTH

In the oral tradition, truth was relational. Something was true because a person of integrity and character said it. Truth was irrevocably tied to relationships.

The harmony and integration that existed between individuals were also linked to their close proximity. The local village or tribe was the center of their known world. Oral cultures lived in their immediate surroundings and had little exposure to areas that required more than one day's travel. Their dialect would be distinct from nearby tribes because of their relative isolation. Living spaces were shared among the village. Experiences were shared and passed down through streams of relationships. There was no such thing as an "individualist." Things happened when you were together with others. Interaction was immediate and intimate.

THE ORAL TRADITION AND CHRISTIANITY

The followers of Christ lived in an oral culture. They lived out their lives in small relational units. New believers would seek out relationship, interaction and fellowship with other (usually elder) members of the group. For its first five centuries, the Church was incubated in oral cultural traditions. The New Testament Church on a local level was a house church. Christians met for worship in small groups and in their homes.[8] "The Christian movement expanded largely due to the conversion of the heads of families, who, in turn lead their entire households in baptism into the faith of Christ."[9]

"Most of the Bible existed first in oral form and depended for its survival on a circle of people who memorized it, recited it, and handed down to successive generations...Even in New Testament times the teachings of Jesus and the stories of His acts seem to have circulated orally until the passing of the apostles and the linguistic transition from Aramaic to Greek made it desirable to produce written Gospels for the instruction of the church."[10]

THE HEART OF WORSHIP

New Testament worship was, of course, also incubated in an oral culture.

One of the central aspects about worship in the first three centuries of the Church was the "Agape Feast" or the Eucharist. Sunday was a workday, and the Christians gathered after work for a potluck meal, known throughout the Mediterranean world as the "Agape," and for the Eucharist (literally, the Thanksgiving).[11]

The highlight, or center of worship, was the celebration of the bread and the wine. It represented the body and blood of the Lord Jesus Christ—the central Person of this newfound faith. The oral culture valued relationship and therefore this act of worship, "remembering the Lord," was a cherished part of worship. In fact, it was the high point of the gathering. The person of Jesus and the remembering of His acts were central.

The focus of the new Christian faith was worship. There were no church buildings; the worship was informal—the home or synagogue was the setting of the worship of these followers of Christ.

The synagogue was often built with a main room containing benches or chairs on three sides, with the seats at the back elevated for those of greater honor. For larger crowds more chairs would be brought into the center area. This configuration was necessary to facilitate discussion and interaction. Worship for the Jews was somewhat interactive and participatory. These gatherings were informal and reflected a great sense of community. There was no official participation by priests or Levites and no sacrifices were offered. The services were orderly but not formal, and conducted by ordinary members of the Jewish community. The Jewish Christians' worship was characterized by flexibility, diversity and intimacy—it was "unplugged."

The Metamorphosis of Worship

The new Jewish believers often sang as they gathered together to worship. The psalms were a rich source of inspiration for New Testament worshipers. In these informal gatherings the believers were encouraged to celebrate in psalms, hymns and spiritual songs. Music grew out of their lives; it reflected the oral tradition of spoken words which kept faith with internal realities. The song was a vital medium of imparting truth.

In contrast, ancient Greek culture tried to remove music from its place in the fabric of life, establishing it as an art form for its own purpose. The value of music no longer hinged on its reflection of truth but on the beauty of its execution. The music was no longer a part of the rhythm of life; it began to be something outside of life and the person. The music was intended to be lifted up and appreciated for its own purpose.

The council of Laodicea, in the fourth century, declared that only the appointed singers who sang from the book were allowed; others should not sing in the Church.[12] Sacred songs and worship began to move beyond the reach of the common people. Only the clergy could sing in choral groups, and a very narrow repertoire of prescribed chants were allowed for the next thousand years. Christian worship music became specialized and an exclusive vocal art form. Melody was considered sacred but rhythm was viewed as inappropriate for worship because it could inflame and incite.

The congregation's role went from being active participants to passive spectators. Music became more difficult and the people could not sing it. They were required to stand and listen to the clergy's performance of musical prayers and melodic worship on their behalf. Clergy became the surrogate for the believer's worship. Priests and monks muttered litanies that only they knew and benefited from.

Although we don't really comprehend what the primitive oral tradition was about, the spoken word still shapes our perception of, and relationship to, reality. Wiesel is right: *The spoken word and the written word are not the same; they do not reflect the same experience.* It is fundamentally different from the written, electronic, digital or any other future medium.

God creates by the spoken word. Because we are created in His image, our spoken words are also productive. Various surveys indicate that a majority of new Christians are brought into relationship with Christ through another person. Apparently, the human voice is a more viable "on-ramp" for the "highway to heaven" than reading books (even the Bible). The spoken word is a better carrier of *life* than the written word; it is more capable of impregnating others with the seed of life.

Admittedly, we don't live in an oral culture. It is certainly true that we don't grasp the power of the spoken word as the first-century Christians did. However, our spoken words still carry the power of life and death (see Prov. 18:21). This power flows from the same creative source that formed the universe.

THEN THOSE WHO FEARED THE LORD TALKED WITH EACH OTHER. AND THE LORD LISTENED.

—Malachi 3:16 *[NIV]*

We can honor and participate in our inherited oral tradition to a greater degree by developing a respect for language, increasing the reliability of our own words, and making sure that our words keep faith with the truth. As recalled by Malachi, we should "talk to each other" more, remembering that our spoken words incarnate power; they still *intervene* in life.

The oral tradition continues.

The Spoken Word 4000 B.C. - A.D. 1500

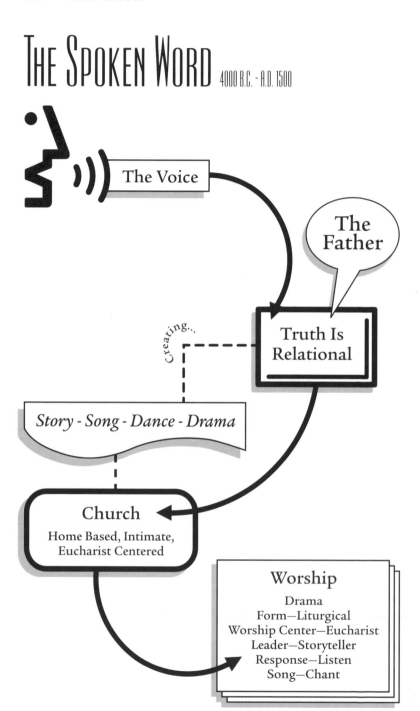

The Voice

The Father

Truth Is Relational

Creating...

Story - Song - Dance - Drama

Church
Home Based, Intimate, Eucharist Centered

Worship
Drama
Form—Liturgical
Worship Center—Eucharist
Leader—Storyteller
Response—Listen
Song—Chant

Notes

1. Elie Wiesel, *Memoirs: All Rivers Run to the Sea* (New York: Alfred A. Knoph, 1995), p. 65.
2. Ibid., p. 74.
3. Ibid., pp. 93, 94.
4. Ibid., pp. 150, 151.
5. Walter Ong, *Presence of the Word* (New Haven, CT: Yale University Press, 1967), p. 91.
6. Carl Hausman, *Metaphor and Art: Interactionism and Reference in the Verbal and Nonverbal Arts* (New York: Cambridge University Press, 1989), pp. 5, 111, 198.
7. "Image: Images and Imagination," *The Encyclopedia of Religion*, vol. VII ed., p. 108.
8. Robert Webber, *The Complete Library of Christian Worship*, vol. 1 (Nashville, TN: Star Song/Abbott Martin, 1994), p. 153.
9. Ibid., p. 169.
10. Ibid., pp. 222, 223.
11. Ibid., p. 145.
12. Charles Fromm, "New Song: The Sound of Spiritual Awakening" (a paper presented to Oxford Reading and Research Conference, Oxford, England, July 1983), p. 5.

CHAPTER SEVEN

THE FIRST WORSHIP REFORMATION

Paper, as an idea and a product, originated in China in the second century. It took about a thousand years for it to reach Europe. By the fourteenth century, paper mills were located along rivers in Italy (the production of paper required enormous amounts of water). Paper was not as strong or as beautiful as parchment, but a manuscript of 150 pages on parchment required a dozen sheepskins! Paper, however, was cheap, flexible, and relatively uniform in size, thickness, and surface. It was destined to make written words accessible to the masses.[1]

Said of many but descriptive of few, it is true that a printer named Johannes Gutenberg changed the course of history. This young German of noble birth invented movable type, the printing press and the special ink that made mass-produced printing a reality. He invented printing techniques and technologies that remain largely unchanged to this day. By the time Martin Luther came on the scene there were twenty-four printing centers throughout Europe.

Within two weeks of Luther posting his *95 Theses,* they were printed and mass distributed throughout Germany (without his permission). Within thirty days they covered Europe. In fact, Luther explained to Pope Leo X, "It is a mystery to me how my theses...were spread to so many places. They were meant exclusively for our academic circle here..."[2]

Gutenberg, a good Catholic, would never have approved of the results of his invention and the spiritual reformation that it facilitated. However, this reformation provided a new structure and had a new apologetic that further expanded the gospel and influence of the Church.

Rex Miller has said that if the oral medium represented the age of community, the printed medium represented the age of ideas.[3] It is not coincidental that reformed churches came into existence about the same time as this new mass communication tool was invented. Gutenberg set off a revolution that allowed individuals to read Scriptures for themselves.

Without the new printing technology would there have even been a Protestant Reformation? Only a century earlier, both John Wycliffe and John Huss initiated spiritual reform and both were authors of powerful documents and movements. The absence of adequate printing technology limited the mass distribution of their works. As a result, their ideas and concepts did not spread very far or very fast. History only considers them forerunners of the Reformation. Would Martin Luther have experienced the same fate without access to a "modern" press?

The world changed as a result of this new technology. Of course, it would greatly impact the Church and her worship.

THE PRINT TRADITION:
THE EYE OF THE BEHOLDER

The first church was born in an oral culture; information and the one who delivered (spoke) it were inseparable. All of life was centered in the local community and its traditions. Gutenberg changed that; his inventions set the stage for a new paradigm within the Church (and, let's not forget, created a base for Western civilization).

In the new communication medium, the perception of information was through the eyes. People were able to communicate thoughts and ideas to large groups of people whom they didn't even know. The perception of information via the eyes created a sense of exclusion and distance. The eye objectifies the word and is inherently discriminating, as it only perceives and processes information it can *see*. The eye is silent.

In the reformed model of worship, which developed in the typographic culture, the focus was on the content of the words. The individual had far greater independence and was, in fact, loosed from his or her bonds to the community. Because of the print medium, one makes contact (albeit less intimately) with a wider range of individuals through (conceivably) mass-distributed books around the world. In the oral culture, impartation came from a core of intimate relationships. In the print medium, personal input is more formal, less relational, and more abstract.

Beliefs and traditions form character in an oral culture. In the printed word culture, character is shaped by concepts and principles. Family and community bonds are essential in the oral tradition—the primary bond of commitment is to the tribe or clan and their expression of faith. It was the faith of "Abraham, Isaac and Jacob" that bonded the Hebrews' oral community. However, in the typographic paradigm there is more of a commitment to an idea or "the cause." In this new print culture, people bonded over doctrine and cause even to the point where these issues separated families. *Individual* validation of truth tends to isolate it from one's organic heritage or culture. One's beliefs are more dependent on personal conviction. The print format transported believers from passing down the faith of the patriarchs and the apostles to merely affirming the faith of the founders (such as Luther, Calvin and Wesley).

This new culture found its faith expressed in commitment to the cause. This facilitated bureaucracy because there had to be "mediating structures" between the individual and the cause. Therefore, denominations were born. Eventually, of course, they become crystallized and unviable; inevitably, there are those in the culture who can no longer accept the "rightness" of the cause. This may explain the institutional entropy which has become more visible within the past fifty years. Some institutions—such as governments and the Church—are living in a paradigm that came out of the Reformation with the invention of the printing press. The business world has long since seen that bureaucracy does not work well in the newer communication-driven cultures that have merged in the last few decades of the twentieth century.

As usual, the Church is arriving at the truth a little later.

CHILD OF THE DEVIL!

John Wycliffe believed in the right of everyone to know the Bible. He was obsessed with helping people know the importance of a personal relationship with Christ. He understood the priesthood of the believer. Driven by a goal of seeing the complete Bible translated into the language of the common person, he wrote feverishly for years, even after a stroke in 1382 left him partially paralyzed. His vision was fulfilled after his death, and this first translation was called the *Wycliffe Bible*.

The students who studied under him at Oxford carried his writings to Bohemia and spread "the Word." John Huss and his followers picked up Wycliffe's cause of getting the truth of the Scriptures to every English-speaking person.

Of course, translating the Bible into the "vulgar" tongue of the common person was heresy; the Church felt the only sacred tongue was Latin. Additionally, Church leaders believed that Christ gave His gospel to the clergy and learned doctors of the Church so that they might give it to the people. A Bible in common English made the sacred Scriptures accessible by masses, the common people, even women! Many in the Church were convinced this was throwing the pearl of the gospel before swine, and this jewel of the clergy was turned into the sport of the laity. The Archbishop of Canterbury, years later, pronounced Wycliffe "a child of the Devil," a pupil of Antichrist.

All of this came about because a printer invented movable type, a printing press and some ink.

THE POWER OF THE PRINTED WORD

Martin Luther had waited a long time to be heard. In the spring of 1521, the time came for his views on worship to become known. The Roman emperor Charles V declared a meeting in Germany (called the Diet of Worms) in order to meet the German princes and take care of Church business. Luther received the hearing he'd requested for years. He was escorted into the meeting and was awed to see Emperor Charles V in person. Spanish troops dressed in their finest uniforms, representatives of Rome, electors, bishops, advisers, territorial princes and others representing many great cities of the empire surrounded the emperor. In the middle of this prestigious gathering was a table with a large pile of books.

Luther was asked if he'd written the books and were there any parts he wished to recant. Given an evening to think and pray about it, the next morning Luther replied, "Unless I can be instructed and convinced with evidence from the Holy Scriptures or with open, clear, distinct grounds of reasoning...then I cannot and will not recant, because it is neither safe nor wise to act against conscience."

The new technology of print communication made it possible for Luther to challenge a thousand years of Church tradition; his use of that technology laid the tracks for the coming train of the Reformation. The printing press thrust Luther and his *95 Theses* into the public arena and created a revolution. By 1500, printed texts of the Bible in Latin, German, Italian, Catalan and Czech appeared. The Bible was spilling into the streets. The authority of the Church could no longer contain or limit the "heresies" of the reformers. The Church leaders were no longer the dispensers of the Word. Anyone who had God's Word, and if they could read, could apply it to their lives—the Word was out!

LOGICAL TRUTH

In this new print medium, those who read what others wrote measured it for relevancy and truthfulness. If it "made sense" or was "logical," then the document and its contents were considered factual and true.

Rex Miller points out, "Logic grew out of sequential characteristics of the alphabet. Writing with the alphabet is the process of assembling letters and then words into self-conscious sequence. Writing allows one to develop a thought one step at a time. Conversely, it is awkward to write one thought in a 'point-counterpoint' format. Logic reaches its destination with greater efficiency. It offers closure to one's pursuit."[4]

Of course, our educational system is still built on the reason and logic paradigm from the print medium.

A SEISMIC SHIFT

In the oral culture, an individual's primary concerns revolved around a sense of place—the personal security which required being part of a community. But the primary concern brought by the cultural assumptions that developed around the printing press was the sense of meaning and purpose; there had to be a "reason" for doing something and being someone. Not having or knowing the "purpose" in life caused one to feel lost. A lack of meaning might be symbolized by depression and despair.

Perhaps that is why in Baptist tradition (a denomination that came out of the Reformation) "finding the will of God for your life" is a strong emphasis. I also, from my Dutch Reformed background, need to know the theological foundations for my experiences with God. *Where is the biblical precedent?* I would ask myself before I could accept it. Do we have to have a "reason" before we have "experience"?

Although the Scriptures are primary in determining our pathway, it is also true that the Lord can do what He wants in the lives of people. It is not weird or unbiblical to experience something before we find it in Scripture. In fact it is a Kingdom principle to experience first. We were "saved" before we understood the theology of salvation. We were "filled" with the Holy Spirit before we understood the doctrine of the Holy Spirit.

WHY DO WE GATHER? HOW DO WE WORSHIP?

In the oral culture, the central reality of worship was the Eucharist; it was relational. The words that Jesus spoke to His disciples, "Do this in remembrance of me" (1 Cor. 11:24, *NIV*), were far more meaningful to those of the oral orientation. The reformed tradition of worship is mostly focused on singing and preaching. The high point of worship is the preaching of the Word.

For more than a thousand years of Christian worship, laypeople rarely sang. Then along came Luther. Other reformers during his time tried to confine and limit expressions of worship. Zwingli banned the playing of organs because he rejected the use of instrumental music in Christian worship. Calvin saw music as a gift from God only for the secular realm. He considered instrumental music "senseless and absurd," forbidding the playing of harmonies. Only unison singing of the Psalms was permitted.[5]

But Luther thundered his response, "I am not of the opinion that all arts are to be cast down and destroyed on account of the gospel, as some fanatics protest!"[6]

I WANT TO TEACH THE WORLD TO SING

One of Luther's greatest legacies was to bring the entire congregation into the act and experience of worship. "Who doubts," Luther wrote, "that originally all the people sang these which now only the choir sings or responds to while the Bishop is consecrating?"[7]

Luther promoted the use of the voice and music in worship by all. He knew that God had a purpose in giving humans the capacity for language, that the gift of song enables the creature to praise God vocally. "We must teach music in schools; a school master must have skill in music, or I would not regard him; neither should we ordain preachers, unless they have been well exercised in music." One of his main concerns was the predominant use of Latin in worship in the public meeting. The common man needed to be able to sing, and hear, the Word of God in his own German language so he could be edified.

The prevailing musical worship medium of this era were the hymns. They were the modern songs of this time. Luther said, "The Devil should not be allowed to keep all the best tenets for himself...I have no use for cranks who despise music, because it is a gift of God. Next after theology, I give to music the highest place..."[8]

The shift from Latin to German-language hymns was slow because of the time required for translation. Poets and musicians were invited and commissioned to produce German hymns and liturgies that would faithfully communicate God's Word. Luther instructed songwriters to use the simplest and most common words, preserve the pure teaching of God's Word, and keep the meaning as close to Scripture as possible. Motivated primarily by a desire for spiritual purity, Luther decided to write his own hymns. Hymnals proliferated so rapidly that many of Luther's hymns were published without his permission.

The songs were "doctrine heavy" in content because the paradigm in this culture focused on principle and purpose. They wanted to remove mysticism and focus on the doctrine of the Christian faith. That caused many of the songs to have a horizontal focus; their purpose was to testify, reason, and proclaim principle. It was in essence "singing the sermon." As a "little sermon" it began to be viewed as the "preliminary" because the main purpose of the gathering, the sermon, was to follow. The singing did not need to be long for it was a proclamation to the visitor and an affirmation to the believer. The song service did not focus on a greater agenda than that of singing songs. There was no need to lengthen it or wait on the Holy Spirit. Remember, this was a "thinking" revival. Birthed in a print-logic culture, there was little demonstration of the "charismata."

Luther was a proponent of equality in worship. "It is pure invention that pope, bishop, priests, and monks are called the spiritual estate, and all princes, lords, artisans, and farmers are called the temporal estate," Luther declared. "This is indeed a piece of deceit and hypocrisy."

He also challenged the idea that only the pope may interpret Scripture. For almost a millennium the Romanists were the trustees and interpreters of Holy Scripture. (Luther argued, "They never learned a thing from their Bible their entire life!")

He also denounced the Roman prohibition of "the laity" from receiving the cup when celebrating the Eucharist.

ENCOUNTERING GOD

The Reformation brought a new emphasis on the priesthood of the believer through Jesus Christ. Unlike the patriarchal model of the oral cultures of Constantine, there was a fresh focus on Jesus the Son and Lamb of God. The reliance upon rituals, sacraments, or the authority of the Church began to diminish. The focus of the preaching of the gospel became more "evangelical." The sacrificial act of Jesus as the Lamb of God who died for our sins was more central. The goal was to see people give their lives to Jesus.

Luther rejected the Constantinian legacy of the Mass as a sacrifice the priest offered to God. In the pre-Reformation period the Mass and the Eucharist were considered the touchstones of worship. The Mass was viewed as having mystery and power. The common man was so removed from the center of worship in the Mass that it was exaggerated in the eyes of the would-be worshipers. Because Latin was not understood, the liturgy of worship carried an air of the untouchable and the mysterious. That, mixed with transubstantiation, caused the common man to see Mass as a spiritual enigma. The Mass was elevated and Christ was more in the background. The common man thought that if he could be physically nearby whenever and wherever the Mass was celebrated then he might find favor with God. Mass had a power over the people and so did the professionals who carried out this sacred drama.

In Constantinianism, encounters with God were in the Mass and more specifically the Eucharist. This is where the worshiper (the ordained priest) touched God. Because of the Reformation, the presence of the Lord was encountered at the hearing and the reading of His Word. Additionally, Luther allowed all communicants to receive the body and the blood of Christ in the sacrament.

In the oral paradigm the Word came forth as a sound. The sound was powerful. The sound was relational; it was inseparable from the One who spoke. It created and nurtured life. It never returns to Him without accomplishing His intended purpose. We are not only recipients of its power, but we also carry the power of life and death in our voice. As noted in chapter 6, we can honor and participate in our inherited oral tradition to a greater degree by developing a respect for language, increasing the reliability of our own words, and making sure that our words keep faith with the truth.

As recalled by Malachi, we should talk to each other more (see Mal. 3:16), remembering that our spoken words incarnate power; they still *intervene* in life. We are also beneficiaries and carriers of the written word. As was true of oral communication, so the written word shapes who we are, because what we see comes from the way we see it.

THEN THE LORD ANSWERED ME AND SAID: "WRITE THE VISION AND MAKE IT PLAIN ON TABLETS, THAT HE MAY RUN WHO READS IT."

—HABAKKUK 2:2 *(NKJV)*

God unlocked the mystery of paper to the Chinese in the second century. More than a thousand years later, the Spirit gave revelation to Johannes Gutenberg. That revelation enabled the Word to rush over the banks of the family and village to cover the earth. The technology gave wings to the Word which God had forged in Martin Luther. The Word dismantled a thousand years of Constantinianism. By providing access to the sacred

Scriptures, it staggered the elitism that locked worshipers out of the holy place. Like a flood surge, print technology leveled ideas and structures and systems that isolated God's people from His presence.

Despite the cataclysmic changes of going from the spoken to the written Word, the typographic culture did not invalidate the oral culture. As scholar John Kennedy wrote in *The Torch of the Testimony*, the Reformation not only facilitated "a return to certain principles of Scripture which allowed not only the individual free access to the benefits of grace, but also a return, in part at least, to the corporate life of fellowship which was a distinctive mark of the early churches."[9] God, in His wisdom and generosity, used a new technology of the *printed* word to bring people back to the benefits of *spoken* word culture.

For more than 500 years, we have lived in a view of the world which has been shaped by the written Word. Of course, it did not destroy or nullify the written Word; it has only increased the texture and dimensions of *the word* in all of its power and mystery. As a result of new communication technology, a print cultural paradigm birthed a worship reformation.

What did the next communication medium bring? Like a rose in bloom, we will see the word continue its expansion through the electronic medium.

THE PRINTED WORD 1500 - 1900

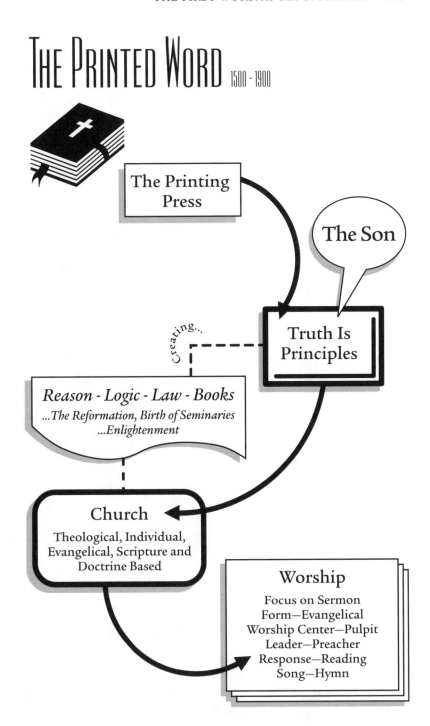

The Printing Press

The Son

Creating...

Truth Is Principles

Reason - Logic - Law - Books
...The Reformation, Birth of Seminaries
...Enlightenment

Church
Theological, Individual,
Evangelical, Scripture and
Doctrine Based

Worship
Focus on Sermon
Form—Evangelical
Worship Center—Pulpit
Leader—Preacher
Response—Reading
Song—Hymn

Notes

1. Fernand Braudel, *The Structures of Everyday Life* (New York: Harper & Row Publishers, 1981), pp. 397-399.
2. Perry Brown, "Preaching from the Print Shop," *Christian History*, vol. 11, no. 2, issue 34, (1992), p. 33.
3. Rex Miller, personal interview by LaMar Boschman, Grapevine, TX: April 1998.
4. Ibid.
5. Paul J. Grime, "Changing the Tempo of Worship," *Christian History*, vol. 12, no. 3, issue 39 (1993), p. 16.
6. Ibid.
7. Ibid.
8. Mary Ann Jeffreys, "Colorful Sayings of Colorful Luther," *Christian History*, vol. 11, no. 2, issue 34 (1992), p. 28.
9. John Kennedy, *The Torch of the Testimony* (Goleta, CA: Christian Books, 1963), p. 137.

CHAPTER EIGHT

THE SECOND WORSHIP REFORMATION

"That's it!" Rex Humbard shouted.[1] It was 1952 and the soon-to-be-famous Akron, Ohio, pastor had just seen a new gadget called television. But like all visionaries, he saw more than everyone else; he saw the potential of a new communication medium. He was one of the first evangelical preachers to do so.

"In 1954 when Oral Roberts took his big tent to Akron, Ohio, for a crusade, his old friend Rex Humbard persuaded him to film three of the evening meetings. Roberts was ecstatic about the results. The programs included not only his sermons but also the 'altar calls, healing lines, actual miracles, the coming and going of the great crowds, the reaction of the congregations.' He believed he had found a way to introduce the nation to the remarkable healing revival."[2]

Roberts jumped into the new medium and his mailing list grew by more than a million names by the end of the 1950s. Billy Graham began receiving 50,000 to 75,000 letters each week during his New York City telecasts. As technology opened new doors, the most creative ministries experimented with new ways to use this exciting new medium.

In 1969 Roberts embraced a new strategy that would dramatically influence the course of Christian television. He focused on producing a new entertainment format featuring talented singers from Oral Roberts University and recognizable Hollywood stars. He wanted to move Christian television from outside the Sunday morning religious ghetto. These programs began to find audiences of 10 million or more. Following some programs, Roberts would receive half a million letters.

Christian ministries became household names as a new generation of television evangelists soared to greater heights in the '70s. Oral Roberts, Pat Robertson, Katherine Kuhlman, Jerry Falwell, Robert Schuller, Jimmy Swaggart, and Jim and Tammy Bakker all became "television personalities."

But why were most of these Pentecostals?

Pentecostals, because of their more existential worship style, seemed destined for this new medium of communication. Their worship had the right "visual" qualities: the action, dynamic singing, and sense of drama that were new and intriguing to Christian America. "They brought a clear-cut, simple theology to a medium that communicated in ten second sound bites. Complicated and nuanced theology belonged to the days of print...'God is a good God,' 'Expect a Miracle'—were memorable television slogans."[3]

The new communication technology of radio and television birthed a new worship reformation—Pentecostal worship. The stars of Christian television in the 1980s were even more sophisticated, talented, and skillful than the Pentecostal pioneers. They became masters in the manipulation of imagery; they ignored theology and went straight for the sensate. It was a sight-and-sound gospel.

Ultimately, of course, the medium really was the message. Taking on a life of its own, television went on an eating binge; it began consuming its own created stars. One by one, several were pulled into memorable performances in steamy "sex, power and money" stories. They were oh, so mesmerizing to watch. The embarrassing exposures of televangelism scandals were exposed in the same medium that created the stars. Like the character Howard Beale in the 1976 prophetic and award-winning movie *Network*, they were simply consumed by the medium's voracious appetite.[4]

THE ELECTRONIC WORD TRADITION: WHAT HAPPENED?

The spoken word was a relational, *voice and village* based medium. The reality of the oral word was inseparable from the speaker; his or her "sound" carried an impartation. As the word moved through the printing press to paper, it became more accessible to the masses, but became "silent." There was no longer a sound to the word.

Television, the primary medium of the electronic word, caused the word to crash through a wall into the realm of electronically delivered sights (eventually with color) and sounds. A television screen consists of several hundred thousand dots. They flicker on and off thirty times per second. In fact, as advertising executive Jerry Mander explains, a television picture never "exists" as an objective reality.

> What you perceive as a picture is actually an image that never exists in any given moment but rather is constructed over time. Your perception of it as an image depends upon your brain's ability to gather in all the lit dots, collect the image they make on your retina in sequence, and form a picture. The picture itself, however, never existed.

Unlike ordinary life, in which whatever you see actually exists outside you before you let it in through your eyes, a television image gains its existence *only* once you've put it together inside your head.[5]

This new electronic word came marching into the human brain one dot at a time and became internally reconstructed as a *pulsating-with-light-and-sound* word! This technology carried a new, unprecedented and unchecked power—the power to electronically stimulate the emotions, reproduce images, and cause people to have an experience by themselves. The sensory response is the nervous system in this electronic medium. "The mind reassembles the sound and images to create a sense of what must be going on. The inflexible pace is unnatural and forces the mind to assemble patterns as though it were speed-reading. There is no pause and therefore it often bypasses cognition."[6]

With television, the word becomes an electronic commingling of sound and light; that marriage creates a significant impact on the emotions. The word travels from the electronic "box" into the ear and eye of the receiver, but there is no direct contact with a "live" person. This causes a dead-medium quality that requires special enhancement by technology to arouse interest. The impact doesn't endure because it does not leave a strong imprint on the memory and actually creates brain wave patterns of a sleeping person. Heavy volumes of images and sounds bombard the mind, fragmenting it and eventually shutting it down.

This new communications technology produced an unprecedented mixture: culture consisting of passive viewers and a concurrent strong commitment to the personality of leaders. For the first time in history "personalities" were created. The medium created people who are "famous for being famous." Prior to this era there were "heroes" but not what we've come to know as "stars." These great luminaries (like Kato Kaelin from the O. J. and Nicole Simpson murder trial) are the by-products of electronic communication. For the first time in history we have "sports personalities," "movie stars," "news personalities," and "music stars." If the "image" of the personality was great enough, they became branded as "icons."[7]

Television and radio completely altered the shape and texture and even the content of the Word. For the first time, communication could be instantaneous to large masses of people. Relatively few people can hear the oral word from the lips of a present speaker. Only one person can read a book at a time. However, because of the new electronic "broadcast" medium, now millions of people hear the same message at the same time and experience the same feelings at the same time.

The stage was set for large-scale manipulation, stimulation and a new truth.

This was a brand-new "experience" and the result was a new way of thinking and a new culture. It produced the cultural phenomenon that includes concepts like the "MTV generation." Like all forms of communication, the electronic word is shaping *who* we are because *what* we see in the world comes from the *way* we see it.

CLINTON AND DOLE

With this new medium of communication came a new reality of truth. The culture began to view or deduct truth in a new way. It was no longer the dominant view that logic, formulae and published works determine what we are to believe.

Although a new medium shaped a new culture and new way of viewing the world, the other mediums and their resulting paradigms continued to coexist with the generation that grew up in those cultures. These concurrent viewpoints are the result of technology. Never before have so many disparate worldviews and "generational" attitudes coexisted in one time period. This has caused a major paradigm clash and subdivided cultures into smaller groups.

For example, because of a new communication era, politics is no longer about ideas; it is about sight and sound. The presidential election of 1996 between President Clinton and Senator Dole was a classic example. Dole, a product of the typographic communication era, tried to operate in the realm of logic, ideology and creeds. Clinton, a true child of the electronic age, understood that it's about imagery; truth is now symbolic and experiential. So, as the "sonar" emitted from each candidate, the cultural "echo" that bounced back reflected a new orientation to truth. That orientation included such features as a rejection of the past and simultaneous craving for some amorphous future. Inevitably, "The Future" won.

THE SPIELBERG SPELL

My heart pounded in my chest as I leaned forward in my chair. The raptors moved quickly around the building and jumped on the roof. *They are in trouble!* I thought to myself. Of course, not only are the kids in *Jurassic Park* in trouble, but because of a new orientation to reality, I am there with them—*I am in trouble.* The same can be said for all the cinematic masters of vicarious experience: *Jaws, Raiders of the Lost Ark, Titanic,* etc.

We now go to the movies to feel emotions and go to church to get goose bumps. The experience determines the impact, quality and "realness" of what was presented. It is true because I experience it is the axiom in the electronic reformation. The existential paradigm caused Pentecostal and charismatic worship to thrive.

THE "WHATEVER" GENERATION

According to Rex Miller, "The prevailing paradigm of this time period could be expressed in the word 'existential.' The standard for modern culture is 'whatever' seems right for you at the moment. It is an existential relationship with truth."[8]

For example, today a minister will often reference historical facts, Scripture or other sources to justify "experience." However, the reality is that the experience comes first and foremost and the justification follows. This relationship to truth and revelation is one result of the electronic culture of television, videos and movies.

For many, faith has become a point of tangibility; it is a response to something one sees, feels, tastes, smells. It is all about personal experience; it does not have to maintain continuity with external measures for truth or faith. For the electronic-word culture—seeing is believing. This is evidenced by the number of "phenomenon" related practitioners of success, spirituality and health that exist today.

Professor Jeffrey Arnett of the University of Missouri-Columbia has studied members of the 45-million-strong "Generation X" (those born approximately between 1963 and 1977 and also referred to as the "post Boomer" generation) and reports that only 15 to 20 percent attend conventional faith communities with any regularity. "Even for people raised in a religious tradition, whose families took them to church every Sunday, they still reach their 20s and make up their own minds," Arnett says. "In my studies, I'm finding very little correlation between their families' religious affiliations and what they eventually come to believe." This is an indicator that the major influence for morality does not originate from the Church, or even perhaps the parent, but from the dominant communications medium—the electronic medium of radio, television, movies and music.

Gen-Xers are steeped in ambiguity. According to George Barna, 81 percent of Gen-Xers do not believe in the concept of absolute truth.

WELCOME TO THE FIRST CHURCH OF WHATEVER

Charter members of The First Church of Whatever are Gen-Xers, however, Church historians may look back on little Baby Boomer Debby Boone as its founder. In the late '70s, this sweet, virtuous daughter of Pat Boone released her first single, a mega-hit called *You Light Up My Life* (recently recorded again by Leann Rimes). Debby, a charismatic Christian, explained that she actually recorded this rather ordinary love song "to the Lord." Although Debby Boone is a Baby Boomer, she captured the anthem of the Gen-Xers with the song's line, "It can't be wrong if it feels so right."

Rex Miller has said that the oral communication culture produced a strong sense of God the Father, that the Reformation placed a new emphasis on Jesus as God the Son, and that the electronic communication era brought a new focus to the third Person of the Godhead, the Holy Spirit. Indeed, the Church which emerged in the electronic era did have a dramatic flowering of "manifestations of the Holy Spirit." Increasingly, the manifestations were interpreted as validations of one's personal relationship with God and of a church's "spirituality"; an expectation of the supernatural became a standard mark of the more spiritual churches.

Inevitably, the sacred space for worship began to be more theatrical. The stages were large for all the musicians and players in the drama of worship. The churches built during this emphasis are large auditoriums with theatrical stages that are high, removed from the people, and of sufficient size to accommodate a choir, orchestra and large area for preaching and theatrical productions; these churches are multimedia centers. Lyrics to songs and announcements are electronically projected on the sides or above the platform via large television monitors or rearview projectors.

The purpose of the gathering in The First Church of Whatever is an event-based experience. The preaching and the praise must *impact* the worshiper. There must be an experience that one takes away from the meeting. The fundamental component is: It can't be wrong if it feels so right.

WORSHIP LEADERSHIP IN THE ELECTRONIC AGE

New forms of "it feels so right" worship began to emerge in the electronic church. The gathering of believers began to be centered around celebration-style worship, audience-relevant preaching and individual response to stimuli (often called "revelation").

Consequently, the leader of worship in this new church had to be a performer. He or she had to be visually invigorating, engaging, theatrical in dress and deportment. The leader had to have charisma and personality. Such a person had to be able to build and "hold the crowd."

Most of the worship leaders that emerged in the electronic church were dynamic and dramatic. Large crowds were attracted to the flamboyant and extravagant displays by worship leadership. The theoretical justification for this style, of course, was that more people can be reached for God. Larger investments in stages, amplifiers, lights, electric musical instruments, manipulated effects and sounds are all part of this approach and attitude.

WORSHIP LEADERS THAT EMERGED IN THE ELECTRONIC CHURCH WERE DYNAMIC AND DRAMATIC. THE THEORETICAL JUSTIFICATION FOR THIS STYLE WAS THAT MORE PEOPLE CAN BE REACHED FOR GOD.

However, little thought has been given to the kind of church culture that results from that approach. Today, the Church values the individual, the sensational and the dramatic;

it is good if it stirs. Today, church and worship leaders have to "stir the people," "get them pumping, get them jumping," and "blow the roof off this place."

SPIRITUAL SPECTATORS OF THE ELECTRONIC WORD

The National Commission on Civic Renewal is a blue-ribbon, bipartisan panel cochaired by Democrat Sam Nunn and Republican William Bennett. After a two-year study, the commission recently released its evaluation of American culture. It was called "A Nation of Spectators." The report concluded that Americans are withdrawing from active engagement and becoming watchers rather than doers.

Surely churches (and most certainly charismatic/Pentecostal congregations), however, are immune to that trend. The notion is that we have the power of the Holy Ghost and we jump to our feet to worship—we're active, not passive. Unfortunately, the National Commission on Civic Renewal may be onto something which even characterizes our spiritual response, too. We must reevaluate and ask: Are we reaching more people for Christ? Are we changing the pathologies of our communities? Are we experiencing a great surge of volunteerism? Are we carrying the life-changing gospel into enclaves of poverty, disease and ignorance?

What we are doing is mostly applauding. The focus is on the eye-ear-emotional stimuli, the electronic impact, the creation of a vicarious experience. There is so little for us to do, so we applaud.

Penetrating the Culture

Pentecostal and charismatic-type churches and ministries have flourished in recent history. They are currently one of the largest and the fastest growing segments of the Church and have brought the experience of the "Charismata." For the first time in Church history, the focus of worship was not the retelling of the story of the Christ event as in the oral and liturgical tradition, or the rational and logical presentation of the gospel of the typographic culture. Today, because of the electronic word, it is the *experience* of God among His people as captured by the manifestations of the Holy Spirit.

Whereas churches of the Reformation emphasized doctrine and theology, contemporary churches focus on "marketing." While it may seem cynical, communication technology dictates that churches today advertise the message or ministry and go for "market share" among the consumers of religious life.

In the old days, when individuals or families moved to a new area, they sought a local church of their historic denominational affiliation. Today, selecting a new church because of its traditional or familial value is becoming less common. People are attending churches because of what they will provide for them. There is a consumerism attitude rampant among the worshipers of the television era.

Market-driven churches are alive and flourishing but some are paying a high price in the loss of spiritual and relational integrity. Inescapably, churches that plan and posture their worship for the camera and the radio audience move away from character and integrity and closer to image and personality. Perhaps it is also inescapable that our society has a prevailing perception that electronic-age church leaders compromise integrity, that the "medium has become the message" and relativized all other issues.

I do understand that just as previous traditions emphasized the Father and Son of the Trinity, the electronic era is presenting the Holy Spirit. However, there is unavoidable damage to the role of the biblical and historical role of the Church on earth when churches ask a skeptical secular society what it wants the Church to be like.

Take "contemporary Christian" music as example. It speaks in the voice of our time and it represents a powerful penetration of the global culture. However, it is also a reflection and celebration of who we are and not of who God is. We're simply looking at ourselves in the mirror. The result is narcissism.

CLOSE TO THE FLAME

Charismatic pioneer Bob Mumford has compared the presence of God among His people to electricity. Electricity can power generators that give light and strength to a city. Yet electricity is also one of the most dangerous phenomena on earth. It can kill with a touch. And so it is with our Lord; we cannot live without the generosity and grace of God, but we should not take lightly that His power and holiness can be deadly. God is merciful and kind but He also kills people who do not properly and responsibly honor the ark of His presence (see 2 Sam. 6:1-8).

With the advance of each new communication medium, the Church has found itself moving closer to the flame of His presence. This is a cherished place. But it is also a dangerous place, because we have a responsibility in honoring and revering Him correctly.

Drawing closer to God's presence brings us closer to His holiness, purity and integrity (which God takes seriously in worship); however, we shouldn't be reactionary against the accentuations on His Spirit that came about with the emergence of electronic communication. The "gifts of the Spirit" became fresh (some say were "restored") in the Church; the words of knowledge and wisdom, prophecies, gifts of tongues, healing, exorcisms and "being filled with the Spirit" all became normal to the experience of the Pentecostal and charismatic churches.

The electronic communication era brought a new focus on the person and role of the Holy Spirit. What Rex Miller calls the "Celebration and Broadcast" tradition is the focus of the worship and theology in the Church upon the Holy Spirit. We have a new understanding and appreciation of the presence of God among His people as the result of the Holy Spirit's personality and activity.

Some of the most popular published books or musicals today are the ones that focus on "experiencing God." The International Worship Institute is the largest "master intensive" organization of its kind for equipping worshipers in the world today.[9] The Institute's mission statement is "Equipping to encountering His presence." Books like *Experiencing God* by Blackaby and musical expressions like Integrity Music's *God With Us* have grown out of the cultural phenomenon associated with electronic communication; they are addressing and filling a valid need for a greater experience with God.

The explosion of the Word into electronic form has generated a desire among people to experience the Lord more now than ever before. This generation of seekers are more sensate, existential in their relationship to truth, and isolated from the reality of objective truth. This present attitude should not surprise us because it's a natural progression from, and perhaps reaction to, the print tradition. The worship reformations continue.

The Electronic Word 1900 - 1980

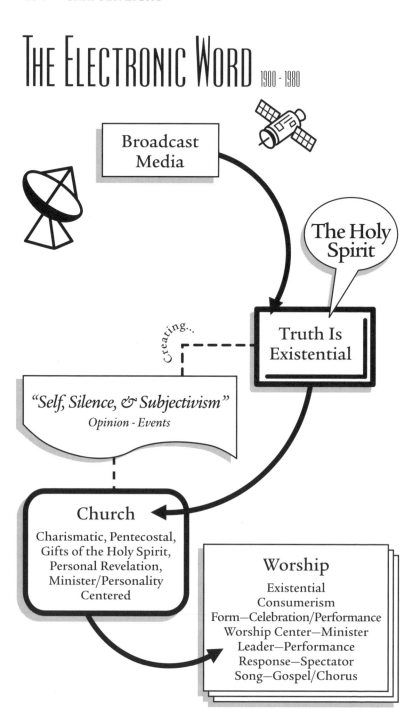

Broadcast Media

The Holy Spirit

Creating...

Truth Is Existential

"Self, Silence, & Subjectivism"
Opinion - Events

Church
Charismatic, Pentecostal,
Gifts of the Holy Spirit,
Personal Revelation,
Minister/Personality
Centered

Worship
Existential
Consumerism
Form—Celebration/Performance
Worship Center—Minister
Leader—Performance
Response—Spectator
Song—Gospel/Chorus

Notes

1. David Harrell, Jr., "Pentecost at Prime Time," *Christian History*, vol. 15, no. 1, issue 49, (1996), p. 52.
2. Ibid.
3. Ibid., p. 54.
4. It is instructive that although he is a television news anchor, the Howard Beale character is—in demeanor, attitude, even speech patterns—an uncanny caricature of a wild-eyed Pentecostal preacher.
5. Jerry Mander, *Four Arguments for the Elimination of Television* (New York: Morrow Quill Paperbacks, 1978), p. 193.
6. Ibid., n.p.
7. Interestingly, a primary component of television sets is called the "iconoscope." It is the electron tube on which the image (icon) is projected and scanned.
8. Rex Miller, "Matrix of Our Cultural History and Future" diagram (research for new book, 1998), p. 1.
9. For more information on the International Worship Institute, write to: The International Worship Institute, P. O. Box 130, Bedford, TX, 76095 or call 1-817-498-9717 or visit their website at www.worshipinstitute.com.

CHAPTER NINE

THE THIRD WORSHIP REFORMATION

Tom, a weary Nashville businessman, steps into the elevator of a Tokyo hotel. Moments later, he drops onto his bed. Although the sun is still hanging over the horizon, his body tells him it's four in the morning. Then, after an hour of sleep, even though the room clock says 7:00 P.M., his brain insists it's time to get up. Caught in the surreal world of jet lag, Tom reaches out for the familiar, the reassuring, the comfortable. He unpacks his note-book computer. Cords seem to instinctively leap to their proper connecting points; the electrical cord finds the plug, the phone cable links the modem to the wall and the world.

Within moments, this halfway-around-the-world son, father, husband and Christian is reading love notes from his wife, responding to a call for help from the brother he is discipling, and inspecting the spreadsheet his daughter, Amy, is building for her seventh-grade Applied Math class. He also has a message from his father; it includes photographs from the ninetieth birthday party of Tom's grandfather. His throat tightens and burns as he gazes into the crystal-clear blue eyes of the old gentleman. He doesn't even think of *how* this photo found him in Tokyo.

Twenty minutes later, having identified the formula problem for his daughter, counseled his disciple, thanked his dad for the picture, and sent a romantic "cyber-greeting" card to his wife, he logs onto his home church's web site. Soon he hears the familiar voice of his pastor. As he makes coffee, he listens to the entire twenty-seven-minute sermon, delivered just a few hours ago. It is crystal clear; he even identifies his own brother's laughter in the audience response to sermon humor.

Communication—more than anything else—defines the way we live.

As Rex Miller has written, the dominant medium filters and fashions society's messages and, therefore, the way we think. We rarely even see this influence. But like the air we breathe, our very lives move within the parameters of the prevailing communication medium. Indeed, when the medium changes, we change.

A medium is a tool, an extension of our hands. It's a tool for communion, connection and celebration. Someone said, "When all you have is a hammer, then the whole world looks like a nail." So, when technology changes from nails to screws, a hammer guy can't function in the new culture that emerges around screws; he's not a "screwdriver guy." But guess what? He'll find some way to work on that screw with his hammer. People, businesses and even churches are like that.

History has known three main media tools:

1. Oral—the spoken word. This tool was characterized by the family, community and "village elders." History resided in the lives of the elders and patriarchs; it was centered around their story and it was passed down. Life was in the community.

2. Typographic—the written word. This era was distinguished by Gutenberg, his printing press, and the Reformation. The emphasis was on logic and reason. It is linear, sequenced and segmented. It facilitated a break from the community to the individual.

3. Electronic—the broadcasted word. Radio and television marked this era. It is an edited medium; sound and sight are manipulated to stimulate and interest the viewer. It brought a new sense of immediacy, mobility, life pace and focus on the future.

Now, we brave the trauma of still another medium, another environment, another reality—*the digital age.* As Tom's routine communication experience in Tokyo illustrates, the digital medium combines aspects of the other three mediums: audio, graphic, text plus data and keeps them separate but allows their infinite combination.

What does the digital age look like? It is the first-time-in-history harnessing of atoms, electrons, quarks and their binary units of information. That harnessing takes the form of compact discs (CDs), calculators, fiber-optic cables, cellular phones, digital video discs (DVDs) and the ubiquitous computer and the global interconnection and interaction of computers into what we call the Internet. Digitalization makes it possible to squeeze, compress, code and

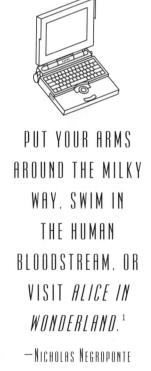

PUT YOUR ARMS AROUND THE MILKY WAY. SWIM IN THE HUMAN BLOODSTREAM. OR VISIT *ALICE IN WONDERLAND.*[1]

—NICHOLAS NEGROPONTE

alter information. It can even be squirted through a cable to be reconstituted at points around the building or around the world.

Think of it: Beethoven sounds better than ever when his music is digitized into subatomic bits of information and then read by a CD player; an optic fiber the size of a human hair can deliver every issue ever made of *The Wall Street Journal* in less than one second; 60-year-old, badly decomposed movies like *Gone with the Wind* and *The Wizard of Oz* can be digitized, repaired, soundtrack enhanced and transferred back onto celluloid film for a more glorious viewing than it ever had in its life.

This wonderful mastery of the bits of information will also challenge the very structures upon which civilization is ordered. Every time history strikes off in a new direction, a new medium births a new polity; a new form of communication creates a new power system. Just as the printing press rendered worthless the previous political structures, the digital age will dismantle and bring in new power structures.

It will reapportion power on a massive scale. Global business already sees this. In fact, the search is on for new alliances of authority, new systems of influence, new patterns of peers. And what they form could turn the Church upside down! Why? Because a digital society is antiauthoritarian. Its diversity blows the circuits of central power. And its self-sufficiency easily survives censorship. Decentralizing will be its ultimate triumph.[2]

THE EMPEROR WITH NO CLOTHES

Successful companies already see the breakup of old top-down, centralized, command-and-control bureaucracies. Global entrepreneurs are already experiencing the dethronement of old monolithic, hierarchic and autocratic empires. Bigger is no longer better; the rigidity of the old model becomes unwieldy and brittle in the complexity of the new faster-is-better world. Overly centralized decisions cause "decision overload" in the rapidity of a real-time environment. And many drowning companies have discovered that huge offices and expensive overhead expedite disaster and death.

The "masters of the universe"[3] and business czars, who used to reign over glass-enclosed and air-conditioned mausoleums, are the new emperors with no clothes and are nearly extinct.[4]

The "morality of computers" is not even an issue; *they're here*. Ethical and moral issues are trying to catch up with a technology that is moving at the speed of light! And no longer are computers about computing. They are about living. They will make the world different and they will make the Church different.

It is estimated that the Internet is growing by 10 percent every month. Negroponte estimates that at this rate, the total number of Internet users could exceed (if it were possible) the world population by 2003.[5] In short, the Internet will become "the center of the universe," predicts Dennis Jones, CIO of Federal Express.

What will this new universe look like? How will it change civilizations and cultures? What will it do with all the naked emperors? What will it do to the Church? What will the Church and worship of the digital age look like?

A CHURCH FOR THE DIGITAL AGE

According to a recent article in *The Washington Times*, about 150 churches, comprised primarily of Gen-Xers, have sprung up around the country over the last decade. Sometimes called postmodern churches, they are fluid, interactive and "virtual." Like digitized photographs, they just seem to "appear" on skateboard ramps, in coffee houses and at punk thrash concerts. Their music runs from traditional hymns to heavy metal.

These churches are absolutely serious about sharing a radical Christian faith in the midst of a society that has rejected the concept of absolutes. They hold to the Apostles' and Nicene Creeds, embrace a "narrative theology," and see the Church as a "counter-culture" in the midst of spiritual and cultural collapse.[6]

The postmodern churches do not represent some new monolithic "church model" of the digital age (in fact, that's the point: there will be no more monoliths). There is a new paradigm Church developing. These churches are not independent, nondenominational or charismatic only. In fact, these designations are rapidly becoming outdated themselves.

The Church is exploding worldwide and can no longer be conveniently categorized according to old wineskins and definitions. The house church movement in China, the explosive churches in Latin America, and the cell church phenomena in Southeast Asia are indications of this. In Buenos Aires, there are churches that meet several times a day almost every day of the week!

Most of these churches are willing to do whatever is necessary to fulfill their mission. They are not institutional; they are indigenous; they have a different concept of time and space in their worship. They meet between cars in a parking lot, or in a warehouse, or simply hang speakers outside their apartment building and have church on the street. How and where they meet causes these churches to be more flexible in spirit. These churches are more spiritual and autonomous. They are large. They are small. They are fast growing, but they're not even in the *Yearbook of American and Canadian Churches* or in the membership directory of the World Council of Churches. The old radar screens don't even see them.

Most churches emerging as part of the digital wave have no relationship to the more traditional church forms or organizations.

Relationships are seen as a spiritual bond, rather than a legal or organizational bond as in the traditional concept.

They may seem charismatic or Pentecostal in appearance or worship style. Yet in the third world, these terms have no meaning to Christians. You may ask a worshiper at the Baptist Church of 240,000 in South America if he is charismatic. He would answer, "What is charismatic?"

Cell-group meetings are becoming a normal level of church life; they are more natural and tend to address the need of community. Casual and informal dress of the clergy tends to remove artificial clergy/laity boundaries. Tolerances of diverse personal styles are common in these ministries, and people seem to be more genuine. The leaders of these churches are usually gifted teachers, preachers, facilitators and are culturally astute.

There is an affirmation of the gifts of the Holy Spirit and an openness to the mystical. Most believe in healing and the power of prayer. They see Jesus *in the midst* of the congregation—not on the platform! (see Heb. 2:12, *AMP.*). The center of worship in these churches is the presence of God. Of course, in the oral tradition, the Eucharist was the center. In the print era, the Word was the focus. The electronic medium focused on personality and experience. In the digital church, the focus may be more on the transcendent presence of Jesus among His people.

In the digital paradigm, participation and decentralization are key factors. The service is not centered on worship leaders, but on the worshipers. Worship leaders facilitate an encounter with God; they don't "do worship" for the congregation.

Some of the core values in the digital communication age are relationship, authenticity, consensus, and context. The emerging culture recognizes the hypocrisy of the "feel-goodism" of the electronic era. Some believe it is and will be radically pragmatic and unforgiving. A primary value is to simply keep the flow of information going and growing. Rex Miller predicts, "Building a grounded ethos for this age will become one of the big challenges ahead of us." That will present fresh challenges for the Church of the digital age.

WHAT IS TRUTH IN THE DIGITAL AGE?

In the oral culture, truth was more relational; in the typographic era, truth was based more on principle; in electronic communication, the orientation toward truth was more existential. In the digital age, truth is more *contextual*; the individual is in interaction with the widest range of possible sources. People have a sense of intimate community while remaining anonymous. Identity is tried on like clothes and tried out in any number of "virtual communities." At the same time, individuals and society have great difficulty dealing with the essentials of human nature. It seems that "the depravity of man" is a given regardless of the communication era.

The oral culture emphasized truth on a relational level where if the holy man said it then the family and village took his word for it. The importance of principle flourished in the print paradigm and the result was if something was published it was considered true. In the electronic age, truth became an experience—"It can't be wrong if it feels so right." However, the digital worldview finds truth in the consensus of the masses. No one has power or control over another because relationships are egalitarian. Truth may be arrived at through the "give and take" of interaction and pragmatic results. That is why polling has taken a new prominence and credence in our society.

Each communication era has produced distinct fears in individuals. The oral society witnessed a fear related to one's sense of place. Survival depended on being part of the family and community. The typographic culture evoked a fear of missing one's purpose in life. The electronic communication medium caused people to have a compelling need for fulfillment. But the core fear of the digital era is a lack of intimacy and belonging. Cyberspace dating, chat rooms, E-mail and other "virtual relationships" represent attempts to find intimacy and a sense of belonging. This may spawn anger, dislocation, aberrant interests and retaliation; if so, life will become increasingly violent.

HOW IS THE TRUTH TOLD IN A DIGITAL WORLD?

In the liturgical tradition, the truth of the gospel was conveyed through reenactment and symbolism. In the digital culture, the truth may be carried in a re-creation, the ability to bring past experience and lessons to current situations and project alternative outcomes. Something like a simulated Disney experience without the limitations of a preprogrammed event.

The impartation of truth in the four cultures is an interesting study.

The primary medium of discipleship in the oral culture was mentoring and apprenticeship. This process was relational and built around modeling the lesson. It engaged all of the senses and used life as the learning tool. Games, parables, riddles, music and plays are many of the tools used to translate the lessons of life. Understanding and wisdom are the focus and the relationship is between the master and disciple.

After the invention of the printing press, the form of education evolved into classroom instruction. The teacher is the metaphoric instructor and the goal was to acquire knowledge. Parables became case studies, dialogue became logic, reasoning and discovery were the focus. The whole motif changed to take advantage of the new technology of print. This more abstract environment allowed for logic, science, the arts and history to flourish. This is why the Reformation was primarily a thinking reformation; as a result many seminaries came into existence.

With the advent of radio and television, seminars became the maturation matrix. Experts provide a narrower skill-based training. The expert uses personal accomplishment as the basis for credibility. These are sometimes called the management or self-help gurus. Achievement is the focus and the educational relationship is fostered between the speaker and attendee.

With the digital communication medium, the message can be a compilation of sound bites, video images, proof text and famous quotes designed to elicit a desired response. The congregation (or disciple) will have the ability to participate, responding to and asking questions, suggesting worship songs, signing up for volunteer work, and even giving offerings!

EXPERIENCING GOD DIGITALLY

Each culture stretches the medium that birthed it (print, electronic, digital) to the limit, magnifying its weaknesses. For example, the electronic age often gave us photogenic, plastic leaders and concert-driven, high-powered, manipulative worship services. Push, push, push, plan, produce and perform. Christian "personalities" came forward, rang our bells, pushed our buttons, hyped and pumped the moment.

However, in the culture that seems to be emerging around the digital revolution, the experience of God's presence will bring a sense of place, the sense of being absorbed. When God's presence is encountered there will be a sense of belonging and finding acceptance. This is important in a culture that is diversified and a family life that is dysfunctional.

As I have traveled North America, I've watched young people surge to the front of churches, crowding the platform, singing and "jamming" to the songs, radiant, enjoying their sense of God's presence and belonging. I see an infectious joy of being part of something larger than themselves. These encounters with God are spontaneous. Songs and prayers are the worshiper's own. Prayers and songs are becoming more of a lifestyle or continual worship than that of prepared pieces that need to be rehearsed and performed by the gifted ones. This praise can be used by anyone, anywhere, at anytime.

BUILDING COMMUNITIES OUT OF SAND

Both Isaiah and the psalmist command, "Sing to the Lord a *new* song" (Ps. 149:1, emphasis added). "True Christian work," says Dorothy Sayers, "is the creation of something new." In short, we were created to create! It is by faith that the people of God have always created a new sense of community.

The digital medium is a community environment: The true value of a network is less about information and more about community. The information superhighway is more than a short cut to every book in the Library of Congress. It is creating a totally new, global social fabric.[7] After all, the computer communicates, and communication creates community. In this community, a "harmonizing web" of individuals is joined in common interests to form intricate networks of interaction and interdependency. If we could "see" cyberspace, it would look like a "knotted fishnet with a multitude of nodes of varying sizes, each linked to all the others, directly or indirectly."[8]

The community has a new global speech. "English will be the de facto air-traffic-control-type language."[9] Or, applying Church metaphors, Don Tapscott writes, "Everybody can use the same hymn book." He continues, "Unlike the Walkman, a technological revolution that created isolation, the next wave will be all about community, communications, and sharing what we know."[10]

Historically, the Church *is* community; wherever hearts unite under the lordship of Christ, we find the "communitarian"

Church. That core truth of the Church will never change. But the *visible forms* of the Church have always morphed into shapes which correspond to the architecture of the age. Although "the church on the corner" will remain, we are also looking at a new medium of church—a Cyber Church—a sacred culture of telecommunications.

Not everyone will "attend" this church. But the paradigm it carries will change the way we view and do church. It will facilitate linkages and networks through a "techno-spiritual" bond, rather than an organizational or legal bond. It could be said that in the truest sense of Paul's famous phrase, this techno-spiritual bond is, for the digital age, the "Body of Christ." This extended "body" creates a synergistic force where two or more come together to achieve an effect of which each alone is incapable. I suggest that Paul would have been thrilled; the Church Universal is no longer an abstract idea.

This new paradigm includes still other forms of freedoms and empowerments: No longer will money be an issue. No longer will buildings, broadcasts, wages, mailings and other outlays be burdens. For "human capital has replaced dollar capital."[11]

Let me give you an example.

Fifteen years ago, Microsoft had almost no capital. Today—built on the power of ideas alone—its share of wealth is greater than that of either General Motors or IBM. This reality of wealth means the Church could also do more with less. It could run world missions once requiring vast resources.

We do not comprehend the possibilities of the digital age! In his landmark book *Wealth and Poverty*, author George Gilder wrote about the dynamic new economy, utilizing

> The world's most common matter, the substance of sand, into an incomparable resource of mind: a silicon chip the size of a fly, with computing powers thousands of

times greater than a million monks adding and subtracting for millennia—an infinitesimal marvel that extends the reach of the human brain incomparably further than oil, steel, and machines had multiplied man's muscle in the industrial age.[12]

Replacing the old industrial-age drivers of success, it is possible that those to whom God gives the power to make wealth (see Deut. 8:18) will charge the front line with nothing but cheap and endless supplies of creativity and...*sand!*

FULL CIRCLE AND MORE

In reality, the coming digital age proposes a return to the "word" of the first century—the oral medium. Was the oral medium intimate? So is the growing multimedia, multisensory world. Was early speech one-on-one? So is a new "de-massified," "on-line," "in-your-face" future. Was there equal opportunity in early communities? So is there equal access in new communities.

Did the oral culture nurture dialogue? So do the enhanced mixtures of high tech and hypertext. Did ancient prophets share inspired visions? So do our inventive cyber-prophets; now their visions can be declared instantaneously and worldwide. Did knowledge move through sacraments and symbols? So today's data moves through super-symbolic cyberspace.

Do we recall shared memories of sacred sages? So will people share memories of the greatest ages. Do we recall powerful moments in ancient life? So shall we know real-time events in future life. Do we recall godly words of eternal and universal significance? So shall we summon global "words" of timeless and spaceless transcendence.

So where are we? What does the future worship look like?

The Interactive Word 1980+

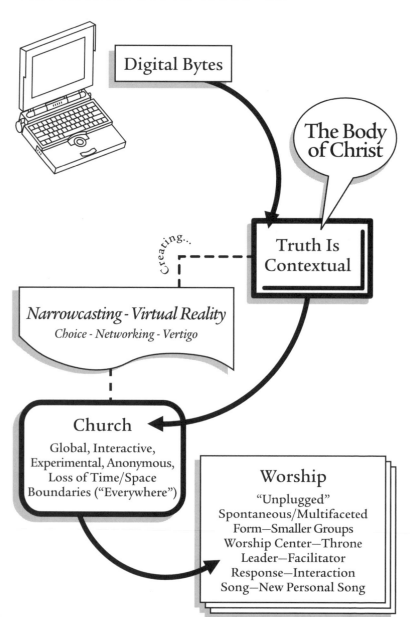

Digital Bytes

The Body of Christ

Truth Is Contextual

Creating...

Narrowcasting - Virtual Reality
Choice - Networking - Vertigo

Church
Global, Interactive, Experimental, Anonymous, Loss of Time/Space Boundaries ("Everywhere")

Worship
"Unplugged"
Spontaneous/Multifaceted
Form—Smaller Groups
Worship Center—Throne
Leader—Facilitator
Response—Interaction
Song—New Personal Song

Notes

1. Nicholas Negroponte, *Being Digital* (New York: Alfred A. Knopf, 1995), p. 119.
2. Ibid., p. 229.
3. Term coined by Tom Wolfe in his novel *Bonfire of the Vanities.*
4. Negroponte, *Being Digital,* pp. 229, 230.
5. Ibid., p. 6.
6. "Postmodern Church Targets Generation X in Seattle," *The Washington Times* (August 12, 1998), n.p.
7. Negroponte, *Being Digital,* p. 183.
8. Rex Miller, "Matrix of Our Cultural History and Future" diagram (research for new book, 1998), n.p.
9. Negroponte, *Being Digital,* p. 45.
10. Don Tapscott, *The Digital Economy: Promise and Peril in the Age of Networked Intelligence* (New York: McGraw-Hill, 1996), p. 234.
11. Alvin and Heidi Toffler, *Creating a New Civilization: The Politics of the Third Wave* (Atlanta: Turner Publishing, 1995), p. 40.
12. George Gilder, *Wealth and Poverty* (New York: Basic Books, Inc., 1981), p. 79.

PART III

NEW MELODIES

It is helpful to remember that wherever we go in time and space, God is already there. He understands—and is very comfortable in—every culture, civilization, and era. He is eternal. He is not nostalgic about the past, frustrated with the present or perplexed about the future. He made and transcends all aspects of time.

We now stand in the beginning of a new medium of communication and, consequently, a new era of history: the age of digital communication. Like smoke, the digital age traces the contours and it wisps in and out of the hollows of the future. This age is significantly singular (a distinct medium from other forms of communication) as were the previous oral, typographic, and electronic eras.

History measures success by those individuals who have the vision to see the future clearly from current events and past trends. Fortunately, those who intimately know and follow the Lord always seem to have an advantage because God allows them to clearly see what is looming on the horizon of the future!

Even now, as Christians who come to understand the new power of digitalization, we can catch a glimpse of tomorrow by the grace of God. Our success in conveying the gospel is being measured by our view of that future.

The future is a new country. Some of us are still in the ship approaching its shore, others are disembarking on the beach, some are now venturing beyond the sand. Wherever we are, we cannot possibly yet describe what the new country is like. We can, however, know that we cannot succeed in this new landscape by relying on the maps or languages of the old country.

Worship is the essential posture of man. How we gather for worship, how we participate in worship, and how we perceive one another in worship is being dramatically altered by the digital age. The new melodies of innovation are stirring in our hearts even now.

WHEN OLD WORDS DIE OUT ON THE TONGUE, NEW MELODIES BREAK FORTH FROM THE HEART; AND WHERE THE OLD TRACKS ARE LOST, NEW COUNTRY IS REVEALED WITH ITS WONDERS.

—RABINDRANATH TAGORE

CHAPTER TEN

FUTURE PERFECT

Like most of you, I have some anxieties about the future, especially the digital future I've tried to describe in chapter 9. I've just become comfortable with the past! As one who has been involved in ministry for a quarter century, I know that the future is not about digitalization, computers, the Internet, or any other technological reality. It is about the will of God.

I also know that we can neither deny nor stop the digital age. It is already here, and we've not yet seen its full expression. Like a hurricane, the forces of history will come crashing into our community. Devastation and death are among the normal results of such force. Then we will go through the typical stages...denial, anger, resolution, acceptance, rebuilding.

We should remember that the Lord permits or causes the hurricane-force winds to alter the landscape of culture, and this is where we live; we have to deal with it. So, I'm trying to give a picture of what the hurricane may do, how to prepare for it, and what the "revised" landscape may look like.

If the following pages seem too high tech, just read them with eyes of faith. And remember, God is already there. He is not intimidated by the future; we shouldn't be either.

EATING ELEPHANTS ONE BYTE AT A TIME

I am concerned that the Church seems to have no grasp of, and certainly no plan for, the digital era. Experts inundate clerics with the latest ideas and ideals for current culture, but few have put forward practices and plans for a future culture. Church-growth experts are still promoting the mass marketing techniques and paradigms that built the electronic church. These soon to be outdated paradigms may not work in this new culture. The new digital generation culture finds this kind of church obnoxious.

Christians have never been called to stick their heads in the sand. After all, God is not a passive Spirit. His presence in history affects far more than theology. He moves in the middle of the raw and real. That's where the Church ought to be. The world is changing, but the Church does not seem to be changing with it. Each paradigm shift is like a new game with new rules. We will either master the new rules or be flattened by them. As good stewards, we must learn to work with new technology and understand the culture it births.

To begin, I would suggest we step outside the conventional "boxes." Allow our assumptions to be tested. We shouldn't be afraid to consider new ideas. In short, it's time to get curious about—and grow sensitive to—trends and events. Like theologian David Lochhead, we should ask tough questions of ourselves and our mission:

What do we mean "proclamation" in a medium that is essentially dialogical? What is "mission" in an electronic community? Is worship possible on-line? In an information society, what is the place of a community like the Church, which values wisdom more than it values data?[1]

We will not find answers to questions like these until we start thinking differently; a new paradigm requires new thinking. In the digital age, new thinking requires us to process information faster and even simultaneously. We can no longer plod along in old analytic ways, because instant facts now coexist in active interplay. Just when we dig up new data, they are suddenly done in by newer data.

Whether the Church likes it or not, God is moving in His own paths and ways. If we want to see where He's moving, we sometimes have to look at the culture, subcultures, and even the fanatics and iconoclasts. They always seem to outpace the mainstream's more sluggish sleepwalkers.

Wisdom has never remained (or, at times, ever even showed up) in the Church. God has never confined Himself to our thoughts—even our "religious" thoughts (*especially,* our religious thoughts). The image of the Church as a gatekeeper for anything and everything important has no basis in fact, Scripture or history. His kingdom is much more grand and majestic than the Church.

Spiritual depth and worldly breadth are not either/or propositions. The Church requires both. So we must discern insight, whatever its source, without contriving distinctions of "sacred" and "secular" knowledge. We must understand the times. That often requires us to seek out the expertise we lack.

The prophetic Church must turn freedom of information into freedom of spirit. She must translate secular information into worldly knowledge and worldly knowledge into prophetic wisdom. An ancient Hebrew proverb commands "Do not confine your children to your own learning, for they were born in another time."

Historian Arnold Toynbee said people groups face crises in one of four ways:

1. They retreat to the past—like turtles.
2. They daydream about the future—like lambs led to slaughter.
3. They become paranoid mystics—looking for demons under every rock.
4. They take hold of the crisis and transform it into something useful.

For some reason, the latter seems best to me.

Unfortunately, the Church usually reacts to change rather than using change. Typically, it labels each new transition as evil. Repeatedly, it enacts the same historic tragedy.[2] Consider Saint Augustine who said Christians should avoid people who can add or subtract, because they had obviously "made a covenant with the Devil."[3] I wonder what he would say about computer programmers.

The Church can and should learn to see both the comprehensive and the particular, vistas and vignettes, and distinguish truth from facts. She can learn to soar above the complex to the whole, yet plunge below complexity to the core; she can ride the waves of a vast ocean, yet measure the speed and direction of the undercurrents.

The Church's leaders must read the signs of the times, know the stakes, and foresee life in the new era. For only then can they set mission goals, strategies for transitions, immediate priorities, and milestones for measurements. Only then can they give their people reasons for hope, roles to fulfill, and victories to celebrate.

I believe in order to transcend, we have to understand the environment we're transcending. Rex Miller echoes, "Once we understand the power of a new paradigm, we can transcend it and affect it prophetically as the Church."[4] We must imitate the sons of Issachar: men "who had understanding of the times, to know what Israel ought to do" (1 Chron. 12:32, *NKJV*).

Understanding the times was no easier for the sons of Issachar than it is for us! When David proclaimed that God has designed and made us to be rulers in Psalm 8:6, he said, "Thou has put all things under his feet." He then went on to examine and detail "all things" as sheep, oxen, beasts, birds, and fish of the sea. Of course, he was only grabbing the details of the contemporary economy. If he were writing today, he would say things like "rocketry, computer science, economic modeling, meteorology, demographics."

Like always, understanding the times is the primary issue; mastering technology and other forms is secondary. Today, we just have to eat the elephant...one byte at a time.

Strange as it may seem, music—with its intrinsic math—may be a primary conduit of information in the digital age. "Music has proven to be one of the most important shaping forces in computer science...the perfect intellectual landscape for moving gracefully between technology and expression, science and art, private and public."[5]

Yet the emphasis of the digital communication era will remain multimedia—mixing audio, video, data and more, culling meaning from many concurrent channels of communication from many dissimilar sensory sources. These multimedia events will certainly surpass anything of the past. They will totally change

IMAGINATION IS MORE IMPORTANT THAN KNOWLEDGE.

—Albert Einstein

the media landscape of the future. Indeed, "whole new art-forms are emerging based on multimedia."[6]

Why? Because computer bits commingle easily. They flow freely from one medium to the other and from one sense to the other. They easily imitate our ability to imagine one notion for another. And in this virtual hall of mirrors, new multisensory media will build ever deeper metaphors of metaphors.

RETURN TO ANCIENT KINSHIPS

Futurists will find one final (and surprising) return to the oral age: one-on-one relations, personal bonding, organic affinities and intimate kinship. The reason? Largely because the mass media (electronic era) has disembodied and "disempowered" the individual. A backlash is forming.

We haven't even seemed to notice how we have passed into a postinformation age where the audience is often no larger than one person—where everything is made to order, extremely personalized and endlessly customized. "I am *me*, not a statistical subset...Classic demographics do not scale down to the digital individual...(for the digital age) is based on a model of you as an individual, not as part of a group..."[7]

As a result, advertisers are targeting smaller and smaller market segments to reach dissimilar customers with greater precision. The "intimate relationship between producer and consumer...will shatter the anonymity of mass consumption, mass politics, mass media. It will be an age of 'in your face' contact harkening back to village life."[8]

And in this village, a modern version of ancient kinship will appear. For in the network, each member is at the center and the center is everywhere.[9] After all, if the digital age has any ethics at all, it's this: "Access and equity should be unlimited and total."

So no one will be left out. Given a will, we will reduce gaps, not increase them.

We see the same trends in the Church. Microchurches are replacing megachurches. Smaller, intimate churches—like those of early Christianity—are replacing anonymous, faceless institutions. Informal, low-tech, oral media are replacing controlled, show business, mass productions.

The "cutting edge" churches of the world are dropping all labels, all classifications and anything that abandons believers to a faceless crowd. But the digital age adds an amazing touch to this change. For the first time the Church can be both large and small, both global and personal.

Of course, information technology—on its own—will not build the Kingdom. Nevertheless, the coming age—for a prophetic church—will surely bring signs of the Kingdom.

BREAKING THE BOUNDARIES OF BELIEF

Douglas Trumbull—the special effects wizard behind the classic movie *Close Encounters of the Third Kind*—designed a theater at the Las Vegas Luxor casino that actually transports audiences into another reality...into visionary realms seen as real events. Trumbull calls it "an experiment in finally going over the edge of a belief barrier."[10]

In short, virtual reality will fully copy reality with an awe-inspiring array of limitless lifelike experiences. Of course it will be misused; new forms always are. It will be burdened with "vain imaginings," godless delusions, empty schemes, malicious caprice. Imagination sins as much as it saves, distorts as much as it discloses, and lies as much as it verifies.

Still, the Church can provide prophetic potential in this new era. *We can model a godly vision in future time.* We can meditate metaphors of a virtual spirit realm. We can make the intangible tangible, the invisible visible, and the implicit explicit. Virtual reality can confirm the Word with signs following.

INTIMATE TRENDS

Global networks are becoming the twentieth-century version of the first-century village—sharing, or doing things for "one another." Perhaps, the digital age may even reempower the family. When television sets become computers, the home will again become the center for work, learning, recreation, fellowship, health care— even shopping and voting. Notice that the home video market is already bigger than the Hollywood movie industry.

PREACHING THE KINGDOM OF GOD, AND TEACHING CONCERNING THE LORD JESUS CHRIST WITH ALL OPENNESS, UNHINDERED.

—Acts 28:31

We even find today's church returning to the first-century model. Believers are joining small, intimate churches. Most churches in America have less than 100 members; perhaps as many as 100,000 churches list fewer than 35 members. Further, most major Christian movements are focusing on *relational* issues. And the glitz, trappings and crutches of present worship are giving way to a more relational, intimate and interactive worship. Truly, we see trends toward intimacy.

Turning the Church upside down releases the pent-up power of grassroots believers. Limits disappear. Walls come down. Individual creativity, interests, decisions and knowledge interact and create value. Spiritual kinship, bonds, fellowships and relationships connect and create community, and the Church benefits.

"Downsizing" the burdensome infrastructures of top-heavy churches also releases resources for global missions. A new agility and a new flexibility allow the Church to grow and change as the world grows and changes. And a new technology and a new paradigm allow the Church to be both large and small in the same instant...global and personal in the same moment.

THE CYBERSPACE CHURCH UNHINDERED

"There are now literally thousands of teachers and spiritual leaders moving across cultural boundaries."[11] Why not the Church? After all, the resources of the Church include the Bible, the Holy Spirit, time, space, and people. All are fluid. Buildings represent our primary constrictions.

But why must there be *any* constrictions to the Word of God? Paul told Timothy that "the word of God is not imprisoned" (2 Tim. 2:9). Sally Morgenthaler said it this way:

> We...love to set limitations on when, where, and how God can work. For instance, God can bring people to Christ in living rooms and at prayer breakfasts, but not in offices, public housing complexes, or bars.[12]

Today's Church stands firmly as a specific community in a specific time and a specific place. Yet that ironclad notion no longer serves the reality of a digital paradigm. In the digital world, space changes to cyberspace. Clear borders between here and there vanish. No longer is there "a place for everything and everything in its place," writes Marshall McLuhan.

Even now, the Internet harbors a "virtual church." In cyberspace, churches will function free of time and space limits. They will be nonterritorial and translocal. Their on-line communities will be dispersed communities, electronic communities, virtual communities—imaginary places where people of like faith join together.

This does not mean all churches will be "on-line." It does mean, however, that churches will come into a new understanding of "space." They may look the same, but they will think differently.

Churches may even look different. The irrelevance of a "worship place" would not surprise the first-century Church. Jesus said, "Wherever two or three are gathered...I AM in the midst of them" (Matt. 18:20, *AMP.*). Moreover, even Jesus in His dialogue with the Samaritan woman made it clear to her not to worship God in a place, but "in spirit and truth" (John 4:23). Churches must look beyond a formal building, a physical location, and old methods of bringing people to a worship function.

CONVERGENCE

A crucial part of this unhindered Church of the future is the principle of convergence—the recognition and blending of various strengths of worship found in the oral, print and electronic ages of the Church.

These communication mediums have allowed forms of worship to merge into an interactive, participatory model where chants, hymns, gospel songs and personal spontaneous singing can all be done in a service of worship. A convergence of the Eucharist (the strength of oral worship), preaching (the high point of reform worship), and the moving in the spiritual gifts (the keynote in electronic worship) may all be brought together in digital reality.

The reason for this is simple: Variety is valued in the digital age of worship; differences are a plus. Using a collage of tools, mediums, gifts and ideas can greatly enhance a worship service experience with God's presence. This can be achieved by "mixing up" the recipe of worship and doing things out of usual sequence. It can go a long way toward keeping things fresh and in helping various churches (Vineyard, liturgical, Baptist, Pentecostal, Black and Asian) from becoming spiritual ghettos.

WORSHIP SERVICE PREPARATION

In the future, the perfect church preparation for worship in some congregations will be different from what it currently is. Today, when we call a worship team meeting a "rehearsal" we are inferring performance. When we only practice songs, the subtle message conveyed is, "We want to sound good on Sunday." The focus is on the externals in such cases—the art of music supersedes the spiritual experience of worship. Although practicing music is necessary, and excellence is important, it is not the highest criteria for authentic worship.

Because of greater spiritual hunger in the digital culture, the focus of worship preparation will be more spiritual. How does the worship team leader prepare for the internal spiritual activity of worship? By praying, reading the Word, worshiping, meditating, fasting, confessing wrongs and asking Christ and others for forgiveness.

We must prepare the place or space of worship as well as our bodies that express worship to God. More importantly though, we must prepare our hearts that create the worship and our spirits that flavor the worship. If we are more interested in the "image" of worship then we will focus on the externals so we "look good" for people. However, if we are more concerned about the "integrity" of worship we will make sure we focus on the internals of worship so we "look good" for the Lord. For He does not look "as man sees, for man looks at the outward appearance, but the Lord looks at the heart" (1 Sam. 16:7).

THE OVERTHROW OF TIME

George Gilder talks about the new economy being defined by "the overthrow of matter." Now, we discover that the future is also about the overthrow of space and time as well. For the limits of time mean little in the coming age. Digital time is NOW. The massive files of past and present pour into each moment with immediacy never known before.

Digital time is flexible, fluid. Networks enable people to work anytime. Companies are now open twenty-four hours a day, because they serve all the time zones of the world! The same immediacy and flexibility already appear in on-line churches. The "Word," for example, is a random access medium, no longer dependent on the hour or the time required for delivery. Even traditional "off-line" churches will soon find the freedom of this new fluidity of time. Increasingly, services will hold ongoing gatherings. Open-ended and less agenda driven, worship will flow like a continuous conversation. And "real time" interaction will be the order of the day.

In Argentina, some churches meet ten times a day, most days of the week. This should not surprise us. In King David's time, teams of worshipers sang, danced, played music and prophesied in rotating shifts, day and night! Many churches today have broadened their worship times beyond Sunday morning to Friday and Saturday evenings and lunch hours, making public, almost continuous worship accessible to worshipers.

All this is good news. It does indeed overthrow the rigid regimen of the clock. Oftentimes we are interrupted or forced into being punctual for things that do not truly merit the demands of promptness. As churches envision a future in a digital paradigm, they will find ways to reach people anywhere, anytime. And in reaching across these frontiers, old borders will begin to blur.

RADICAL FELLOWSHIP

The Church of the future will also cross over those grievous cultural cleavages—the borders between "us" and "them." It will transcend its own myopic ways and embrace true diversity. I believe the digital word will help to break down artificial and contrived walls. The digital revolution—like rock music—appeals to every culture. It thrives on diversity. It honors individuality.

In the past, divisive national and ethnic forces too often characterized the Church. Without apologies, missionaries projected the non-Christian world in their own cultural image. In the past, difference was discouraged and sameness was encouraged.

Today, though, we are being forced to consider networks and to question some of our authoritarian assumptions. Increasingly, churches are adapting forms of worship unlike their historical traditions. Recent polls reveal that two-thirds of the unchurched will only accept a "personal," "noninstitutional" church experience.[13]

It's clear the Church of the future will be less intimidated by cross-cultural meanings, multicultural expressions, and even countercultural idioms. After all, Christianity began as a countercultural movement—at odds with the prevailing view. It was also inclusive—embracing everyone. In truth, it was a *radical* fellowship. Paul said that, in Christ, "there is neither Jew nor Greek...slave nor free...male nor female" (Gal. 3:28). After 2,000 years, could it be that Paul's vision is returning? Global Church growth wildly crosses cultural borders and ignores denominational labels.

The digital communication era will, in fact, "radicalize" our views of truth, spirituality, worship and many areas of our life and culture. New themes will evolve as we see new and old trends emerge.

But what will the worship of tomorrow look like?

Notes

1. David Lochhead, *Theology in a Digital World* (Etobicoke, Canada: United Church Publishing House, 1988), p. 64.
2. William Irwin Thompson, *Coming into Being* (New York: St. Martin's Press, 1996), p. 151.
3. Alvin and Heidi Toffler, *Creating a New Civilization: The Politics of the Third Wave* (Atlanta: Turner Publishing Company, 1995), p. 35.
4. Rex Miller, lecture at the International Worship Institute, 1996.
5. Nicholas Negroponte, *Being Digital* (New York: Alfred A. Knopf, 1995), p. 222.
6. Don Tapscott, *The Digital Economy: Promise and Peril in the Age of Networked Intelligence* (New York: McGraw-Hill, 1996), pp. 61, 62.
7. Negroponte, *Being Digital,* pp. 163-165.
8. Tapscott, *The Digital Economy,* p. 41
9. Miller, unpublished notes.
10. Howard Rheingold, "Douglas Trumball's Big Budget Debuts in Las Vegas," *Wired* magazine, (1.05, Total Immersion Feature, November 1995), n.p.
11. Thompson, *Coming into Being,* p. 261.
12. Sally Morgenthaler, *Worship Evangelism* (Grand Rapids, MI: Zondervan Publishing House, 1995), p. 79.
13. Ibid., pp. 235-238.

CHAPTER ELEVEN

THE LAND BEYOND THE BITTERROOT

One of history's greatest endurance and exploration stories is the Lewis and Clark Expedition. The purpose of the trip was to find a transcontinental water route, the mythical "Northwest Passage." Although it didn't exist, Lewis and Clark found much more; they discovered the true majesty and extremes of the uncharted land "beyond the Bitterroot" River. Even more, they saw the future; they caught a glimpse of the paradigm-shattering effect of the sheer magnitude, topography, weather, people groups and new economic possibilities that would define the next century of American expansion and commerce.

Yet that glimpse of the future nearly killed them. Weather, hunger, illness, exhaustion and the natural defenses of the indigenous peoples all brought them to the very edge of survival. Perhaps the most harrowing and life-threatening part of the journey was the mountains beyond the Bitterroot. It was like God was making the point that stepping into the future is no small issue.

Sometime in the morning of August 12, 1805, the Lewis and Clark Expedition reached the top of a pass on the Continental Divide near the border of Montana and Idaho. At that moment, they became the first Americans to behold the majestic, indescribable, terrifying mountains of the great Northwest. "With Lewis's last step to the top of the Divide went decades of theory about the nature of the Rocky Mountains, shattered by a single glance from a single man."[1]

Today, almost two centuries later, I believe we are approaching another summit, revealing another panorama that will shatter many traditional theories about where the Lord has destined the Church to go.

As one who has traveled the world for the last quarter century, I do believe we are approaching a *spiritual* continental divide. It is a watershed which separates the creeds, assumptions, expectations, patterns and ideas of the past from those of the future. It is no small thing to cross that divide.

In this book we have looked at the condition and future of the Church in a rapidly changing environment. We've examined the influence of the various communication eras and paradigms. The historic trail of faith, walked by generations of our ancestors, has led us to this spiritual vantage point. Let us consider—through eyes of faith—the rugged expanse before us.

GOING ON OR TURNING BACK

Once the Lewis and Clark Expedition actually moved into the mountains, they found themselves pushed to the limits of endurance. They weren't sure they could even cross such an endless and impossibly rugged mountain range. According to Stephen Ambrose, they "had reached the breaking point." But going back was also impossible. It was truly a life-and-death crisis. Finally, they found resolution for the future: "They had to go on. But to do so required desperate measures."[2]

Many churches today are caught in the same crisis; they are not at all sure they can survive in the new terrain, but they can't go back either. They don't know what to do. It is, in fact, a crisis of faith. Some would rather reminisce about the land back *behind* their Bitterroot River where they had more pleasant ventures. Others are thrashing around, begging God for a surefire "model" that will guarantee success in traversing dangerous territory. Still others have developed ministries devoted to warning others about the "bad times to come."

Ultimately, the future is about faith. Are we ready to turn loose of our traditions, viewpoints and comfort zones? Are we prepared to abandon the safety of our theological and cultural nests? Do we really trust God? If so, perhaps we are ready to proceed into the future like those who "did not love their lives so much as to shrink from death" (Rev. 12:11, *NIV*). One of the first results born from real faith is the development of a right attitude toward our lives. When we settle that our lives are not our own, and are in fact to be risked for the sake of Jesus Christ, only then are we ready for the future.

GETTING BEYOND REACTION

It is important to grasp an accurate view of the typography of the land beyond the Bitterroot. We must learn to distinguish between Church folklore and the great Christian traditions. Today, more than ever, we are seeing the breaking down of denomination barriers among Christians. We are being enriched, cross-pollinated and impacted by each other, and all Christians are better for it.

We must be open to laying aside the emphasis on the quirks, preferences, rituals and behaviors that mean so much to our particular group. Brian D. McLaren points out in his book, *Reinventing Your Church,* "Our sectarian traditions—our distinctive doctrines, our denominational histories, our proprietary heroes, our characteristic disciplines, our idiosyncratic moral codes, our private art museums—were being used up, and we see ourselves going broke."[3]

I really believe the Church of the future will have a worship and environment that has a shared and cross-Christian cultural environment. Our paradigm must change if we do not want to be left behind in a small world—an isolated spiritual ghetto of our own creation.

Marching at a Marilyn Manson concert, with the ludicrous idea that we will influence Manson and his fans, will not change our culture (or Manson). In fact, protesting *itself* reveals a grossly outdated paradigm still lying around in the rubble from the electronic era.

THE FUTURE OF WORSHIP IS ABOUT PARTICIPATION

In "the land beyond the Bitterroot," the true worship has become almost nonexistent. Several factors lead to the demise of authentic worship where worshipers become mere spectators. These elements include:

1. Worship leaders do not let the congregation know what is expected.
2. Worship leaders/teams are not focused on finding the presence of God.
3. Too many worship leaders see "parts" of worship rather than the whole.
4. People are not comfortable with the style of worship.
5. Too much activity on the platform.
6. The songs are not known.

7. The songs are not singable.
8. Sound systems are too loud.
9. Leaders do not model vibrant worship.
10. Little biblical teaching on the role of the congregation.

New Testament worship was simple and personal; it empowered the worshiper. It was informal; God was initiating a two-way relationship. It was about the Christ event—the epicenter from which all the facets of worship proceed. Jesus superseded the Old Testament institutions. He was "greater than the temple" (Matt. 12:6) and the ultimate sacrifice.

Jesus encouraged individual participation and "lifestyle worship" by teaching us to "worship in spirit and truth" (John 4:24), and to love God with all our heart, soul, mind and strength (see Luke 10:27, *NIV*). Paul encouraged participation by saying, "I want men everywhere to lift up holy hands in prayer" (1 Tim. 2:8, *NIV*). New Testament worship empowered worshipers to fully participate in public and private worship.

FUTURE WORSHIP *UNPLUGGED*

Just as the "MTV Unplugged" concerts feature small intimate audiences, acoustic instruments, and greater intimacy and engagement, I believe the worship paradigm of the future could be called "worship unplugged." It will be decentralized, with fewer leaders, and more participation by all worshipers. The center of worship will move out into the midst of the people. Platforms will be lower, smaller, and often nonexistent.

Rex Miller believes worship will often be an ongoing gathering, "hosted" by people who are more facilitators than leaders; it will allow real time interaction, break-out groups and rooms for Body ministry.

Church strategist Bill Easum says we are moving into an era where worship is "not based on the printed page, sixteenth-century music, and a culture that embraces Christianity." The new worship will be more participatory, more relevant and real; "seekers" will be drawn into the experience with little effort by the leadership. "Unplugged worship" will be *meaningful and empowered* worship; that is precisely the cry of Christians in every denomination.

A POWER SHIFT FROM PLATFORM TO PEW

Let's face it: The eyes and ears of the Lord are on individual hearts, not on the stage, technique, nor the "plug-ins."

Unplugged worship will be characterized, in part, by a cohesion of worship rather than a series of disconnected happenings. The journey of worship should move consistently and cohesively toward an encounter with the Presence. It should not be force-fed, jerky, interrupted and disjointed, but fluid and ascending as we come closer to the Lord. Linking the different events of the service together in one seamless thread will be a greater priority in the future.

I believe worship in the future will provide many options for worshipers. They will be able to enter worship at their own pace; it will not be directive and coercive. Freedom to choose a personal pace and response should and will be extended to worshipers. This will facilitate a greater sense of community and freedom to respond to God in a way each worshiper feels is best for them. They should also have the option not to participate at all without being made to feel conspicuous.

NEW COUNTRY, NEW LANGUAGE

As we move into the new land of worship, we will be faced with the need to learn a new language—a new way of communicating God's truths. What will the new language sound like?

The German theologian and martyr Dietrich Bonhoeffer put it this way:

> It too will be a new language, perhaps quite nonreligious, but liberating and redeeming—as was Jesus' language; it will shock people and yet overcome them by it's power; it will be the language of the new righteousness and truth, proclaiming God's peace with men and the coming of His kingdom.[4]

Brian McLaren, in his book *Reinventing Your Church*, also addresses the new land and new language issue:

> Our words will seek to be servants of mystery, not the removers of it as they were in the Old World. They will convey a message that is clear yet mysterious, simple yet mysterious, substantial yet mysterious...Our words will be less religious, more common, more earthy.[5]

Perhaps the language of the new land will be more like the words of Jesus, conveying parables, proverbs, metaphors and allegory; the new language will feature poetry, stories and song.

Our cognitive culture often deceives itself with "literal" words. And we delude ourselves with their literal meanings. A true "word"—an oral word—does not limit itself to mere *information*. It speaks, instead, a specific message to a specific person at a specific time. It attracts us with something beyond the "word" itself. It lures us with something very desirable, attractive and meaningful. And great thinkers agree this attraction proves its truth.

Inspired biblical writers, for example, were creators of comparison and contrast; they were artists of analogy and affinity and virtuosos of similarity and similitude. In short, they spoke the language of sacred metaphor. As a result, most of the prophetic books in the Bible are lyric oracles or poetic songs.

In short, oral words were "not written with ink," Paul said, "but with the Spirit of the living God, not on tablets of stone, but on tablets of human hearts" (2 Cor. 3:3, *AMP.*).

So, the digital medium brings *a new word*—"linking concepts to one another in startling ways...building up amazing hierarchies of inference...spawning new theories, hypotheses and images based on novel assumptions...(and developing) new languages, codes and logics."[6]

It doesn't matter whether the medium is binary digits or Balaam's donkey (see Num. 22:21-33). God speaks through it anyway. For a true "word" is any place where God's Spirit speaks to our human spirit.

NEW FORMS OF MEETING

The focus of congregations in the new land will be the presence of the Lord among His people. This will represent a significant change from the center of worship in the oral culture—the Eucharist; and in the print culture—the preaching; and in the electronic—the charismata. I believe there will be a stronger desire to see God's revealed presence in all the actions of worship. Program and entertainment will not satisfy anymore.

The throne of God is evidenced when we praise Him according to Psalm 22:3. His presence is evidenced as He is "enthroned" on the spontaneous praises of His people.[7]

More and more worshipers will not want to go home from worship services without touching the transcendent presence of God. A recent survey of worshipers revealed that 80 percent have no sense of God's presence in their public worship services.

I believe the new worship gatherings in the new land will be participatory, real, and infused with a sense of natural community.

They will not be building-centered nor event-driven. Less is more; small is beautiful. After all, the whole thing started with individuals, then moved to families and finally to neighbors; personal bonds formed from small groups that met in homes. Historically, the home has been a better facility for relationships than cathedrals and temples.

The focus of worship in the new gatherings will be—not the Eucharist (though important), not even the preaching of the Word (though important)—but the Lord among His people.

NEW VALUES

Some of you will react defensively toward the idea of "new values." So let me qualify this (so you can get down off the ceiling!): Values come in two boxes—one is marked "eternal" and the other "temporal." We are gathered around the One who is eternal and unchanging. His values cascade out of Heaven. Nevertheless, culture always grows up around each new era; people inevitably develop certain unique temporal values. Worship in the new land will be no exception. The following outlines some of the *temporal* values which will distinguish worship in the new land.

- **Flexibility** will certainly be a hallmark of the new digital paradigm; smaller units (bytes) can be squeezed, broken down, reconfigured; it is fluid rather than solid. This new form of communication lends itself to a greater flexibility of ideas, teachings and services than were possible in the typographic and electronic eras.
- **Diversity** will be a vital distinctive of the future Church and her worship. Ethnic, economic, educational and cultural *differences* will be more accepted and appreciated. As a result, worship will find a new level of freedom and beauty of expression.

- **Alliances and "knitworks"** will be more valuable to churches in the future.
- **Multiexperiential activity,** another value made viable by digital technology, will be the norm in the new land. For example, "normal church life" will feature simultaneous activity, almost like a market bazaar; an ongoing expression of worship, praise, body ministry and exhortation.
- **Spirituality** is and will continue to be "in." The cold impersonal feeling of the digital world creates within people a passion for the mysterious. The culture of the future will have a nonjudgmental faith that is naturally drawn to spiritual issues. The only time such people would be resistant to a spiritual point of view is when that view is openly critical and judgmental of others.
- **Interactivity** is another core value—every person plays an important part and is encouraged to contribute to the whole experience. "When you assemble, each one has a psalm, has a teaching, has a revelation, has a tongue, has an interpretation. Let all things be done for edification" (1 Cor. 14:26).

This famous Pauline instruction lists the verbal manifestations of the Spirit that should occur in the corporate gathering. Gordon Fee says, "The latter three are Spirit-inspired utterances, and are therefore spontaneous." Fee goes on to say, "What is striking in this entire discussion is the absence of any mention of leadership or of anyone responsible for seeing that these guidelines were followed...The Holy Spirit is understood to give basic leadership to the worship of the gathered body."[8]

Worship will become more interactive between each of us and with the Lord. Most of us "have had it" with professionals *doing the worship* for us. We need to wake up! All believers are authorized to be active participants in the public and private worship of God. Each Christian supplies a necessary part that flavors the reality of authentic worship.

NEW UNDERSTANDINGS WHERE JESUS IS IN WORSHIP

For worshipers to think they should sit in the front in order to be "close to the anointing" reveals an antiquated worship paradigm—*Jesus is not in the front of the gathering.* Jesus isn't even on the platform during worship because He's not a performer. He is in the middle of the congregation.

God dwells in the praises of His people (see Ps. 22:3). He dwells in the sanctuary where the praises, thanksgivings and sacrifices of His people are continually offered. The praises of all His people in the sanctuary are the throne on which God sits. He who finds the center where praise is celebrated seems "to dwell in the midst of praises...He was surrounded by those who praised him."[9]

Jesus sings His worship in the middle of the congregation. But we see Jesus saying, "I will declare Your name to My brethren; in the midst of the assembly I will sing praise to You" (Heb. 2:12, *NKJV*). The picture here is that Jesus worships the Father in song, not in front of the assembly of believers, but in the middle. New Testament scholar A. T. Robertson says that this assembly (*ekklesias*) is a local body of the general body of Christ. Nevertheless, Jesus participates in this public worship not from the front but the middle.

Another Scripture confirms this. "For where two or three are gathered together in my name, there am I in the *midst of them*" (Matt. 18:20, *KJV*, emphasis added). Jesus is not "at the front" but "in the middle." He is relational and more interested in "interaction with" people than "productions of" people.

God's presence amid His people is clearly seen when the apostle John recorded in Revelation: "These are the words of him who holds the seven stars in his right hand and walks among [in the middle] the seven golden lampstands" (2:1, *NIV*).

Moreover, where God's saints are His living sanctuary the Scripture declares, "For the LORD has chosen Zion, he has desired it for his dwelling: This is my resting place for ever and ever; here I will sit enthroned, for I have desired it" (Ps. 132: 13,14, *NIV*).

Jesus "hangs" with the brothers because Jesus is relational. His leadership style is more in the Hebraic model of mentoring than the Greek art form or performance, He is teaching by being present and speaking to individual hearts on a personal level.

NEW LEADERS

Jesus is back; the age of the self-promoting professional is over!

As surely as the Berlin Wall collapsed, the age of the ego-driven, selfish, risk-averse leader is crumbling into dust. The crises that will swirl around the millennium change will "level the playing field" of leadership. The arrogant, unreliable, insensitive, injurious "misleaders" will fade away.

The future will be an age for humble, sensitive, caring, selfless leaders who have been to the Cross. They will not be impressed with themselves or any other manifestation of carnality. They will find safety in mutually dependent relationships. They will be prepared to lay down their lives for their wives, families, associates, constituents, and even for entire communities.

The new leaders will understand the beauty of synergy. Synergism describes the effect or value of the whole as greater than the sum of the parts. For example, the pastor, worship leader and musicians each have a distinct value, but when blended together by a common focus their contributions take on increased synergistic value. Church leadership functioning as a team is a critical element in the future Church. It is a more balanced, broader and safer method of leadership. This style of leadership will empower others to be involved in the direction the Church is going.

Above all, the leaders in the future will understand that God has created people for *His* purpose. Those who come to the Lord are drawn and empowered by Him for that purpose. Leaders must understand that believers aren't *their* people; Christians are the sheep of *His pasture*. Each believer is holy to God. A leader has the responsibility and joy to discover and draw out the holy gift that God has given to that individual.

Worship leadership will eventually be transformed into worship facilitators. These facilitators will provide the following:

- **Facilitators have a high standard of ministry.** They give attention to detail, are creative thinkers and are not afraid to be stretched. People connect with God in worship better when they are not coerced, intimidated or commanded, but coached in a caring way.
- **Facilitators give attention to details in those they lead.** They notice things others have missed. By being alert and sensitive, facilitators help team members correct mistakes and discover the true fountains of purpose behind their actions.
- **Facilitators help people get where they want to go.** They do not change their gift or purpose, but merely assist in drawing out that purpose. Facilitators assess where a person is with the Lord and where the Lord wants him or her to be. The facilitator becomes a tool to help the person complete the journey between those two points. Sensitivity (to the Lord, the people and the process) while listening to and surveying the worship is absolutely critical. It is "misleadership" to close our eyes and indulge in private worship without regard for others.

· **Facilitators will call forth and shape the worship.**
Worship will be driven to be one great interactive experience where "every joint" (Eph. 4:16) will support the worship experience. This interaction will be natural and not coerced. The day of "drill sergeant," "cheerleader" and "sing along with Mitch" worship is coming to an end.

Let us listen for the Lord's song in this strange land of the future. Let God arise among the people.

STORYTELLERS

Storytelling, that ancient form of communication that was the strength of the oral culture, should be part of the new leadership style. The spoken word communicates more than information. It conveys *spirit* ("breath").

Worship is living and orally communicating in song, sermon and sacrament, the story of the One who changed our story. In recent years, evangelism and worship have tended to approach communication through a variety of methods: the *program method* of structures and planned events; *psychological methods* concentrating on people's "felt needs"; and the *intellectual method* of reason and logic. However, the *narrative method* focuses on the *story* of God.

A logical, linear, rational approach to simply making outlined points does not connect with the human heart in the same way as does the story. Leonard Sweet, dean of the Theological School of Drew University, says, "Ministers are story doctors. We help people with their problem stories and painful stories and which stories to keep and which to create."

Leighton Ford said, "The second most common reason that people become Christians is that they hear the story of God. The third most common reason is that they hear another's story." The gospel story changes people's lives when it is told authentically and realistically.

Jesus rarely taught without telling stories. It is significant that "postmoderns" reject dogma but that they don't reject stories. The people of the new land do not want us to draw conclusions for them in our telling of the story; they are perfectly capable of making the application.

We just need to tell, preach and sing the story of the Christ event. Just tell the "old, old story"![10] It will never lose its power.

NEW WORSHIP MODELS?

Recently, a leader of historical proportions, a man who was a founding part of a significant twentieth-century movement, made a startling admission. Over a private dinner with friends, he admitted that he didn't *do* anything to be used of God, or to even be "in the right place at the right time."

"I didn't prepare my heart, I didn't seek out successful models; in fact, I wasn't even looking for anything. I and the other brothers simply walked into a room and God met us."

Today, many are spending millions, running across the country and around the world obsessed with finding successful church and worship models. It is perhaps symptomatic of our age that we just want to copy what someone else did. Because of our busyness and our insecurities, most of us just want to "scan" someone else's work into our computer, so we can get on with it. We reduce everything to checking out the Willowcreek, Pensacola, Baton Rouge, Buenos Aires, Vineyard, Korean and Seeker-Sensitive models. After all, to seek God for a format, well, we're too busy. Trust Him? Too much risk of failure.

But darn it, God just doesn't seem to bless cloning visions.

There is no evidence that David looked for the "Moses

model"! I don't even think it would be accurate to say that Paul "copied" the Jesus model. (I can see a religious mob brewing on that one!) Nevertheless, the truth remains that there is very little we can do to get God to make us successful. He just seems to show up at various times and places in history. How, why, when or where are genuine mysteries.

My advice is to seek God, fill up your place, be responsible, enjoy the journey. Love, care, honor, give, work. Give *your* heart completely to the Lord. The best advice I can give for surviving and leading in "the land beyond the Bitterroot" is found in 2 Chronicles 16:9:

> For the eyes of the LORD move to and fro throughout the earth that He may strongly support those whose heart is completely His.

Notes

1. Stephen Ambrose, *Undaunted Courage* (New York: Touchstone, Simon & Schuster, 1996), pp. 266, 267.
2. Ibid., p. 294.
3. Brian D. McLaren, *Reinventing Your Church*, (Grand Rapids, MI: Zondervan Publishing House, 1998), p. 52.
4. Dietrich Bonhoeffer, *Letters and Papers from Prison* (New York: Macmillan, 1971), p. 300.
5. McLaren, *Reinventing Your Church*, p. 90.
6. Alvin and Heidi Toffler, *Creating a New Civilization: The Politics of the Third Wave* (Atlanta: Turner Publishing, 1995), pp. 36, 37.
7. Psalm 40:3 uses the same Hebrew word "tehillah" for praise. It is an original song that has never been sung. It is that song that God said He would sit on as a throne.
8. Gordon D. Fee, *God's Empowering Presence* (Peabody, MA: Hendrickson Publishers, 1994), p. 249.
9. Barnes's notes, Biblesoft: PC Study Bible Software, 2.1, n.p.
10. William Gustavus Fischer, "I Love to Tell the Story" taken from the poem, *The Old, Old Story* by Arabella Katherine Hankey; *Joyful Songs*, nos. 1 to 3 (Philadelphia: Methodist Episcopal Book Room, 1869), n.p.

HOW SHOULD WE THEN WORSHIP?

I trust that you have caught a glimpse of the future. I hope this book is helpful to that process.

Because I am known as a "worship doctor" and "worship leader," I am often asked for advice on better ways to "do worship." So, I want to share some personal thoughts about navigating into the future of worship.

In building for the future, wisdom always recognizes that major changes will come. Of course, sometimes we have to make "tentative" and "tactical" changes as we wait for His change. But it is important to realize that going on with God will take us through a complete metamorphosis. *We are not what we shall be.* I am reminded of Rex Miller's comment, "We do not originate or even manage real change; it always invades from the outside."

I would suggest that for those in leadership positions, *navigating* change will require developing a strong leadership team of risk takers. I would also suggest that the team spend time together in personal interaction, not just programmatic stuff. Stretch their paradigms while you validate their worth.

Declare a clear and vibrant vision. Often leaders fall into a "default mode" of pushing people rather than leading. I've done it too. Let me tell you, that is like pushing a log chain! It is so much better to hear what God is saying, declare that to the people (and society) and watch the people "fall in line behind the vision."

The possibilities of fulfilling the mission the Lord has given us will always cause people to become more active as participants and focused upon goals ahead. However, be careful to move slowly when implementing a sense of urgency to a new vision.

Many church leaders attend conferences on the latest new "worship thing" going around, return home with gathered momentum, spark a 180-degree change in the church, only to watch the new vision crash into a ditch! When changes are made abruptly without careful explanation and slow implementation, the people, like sheep, become disorientated and wild (maybe that's the reason the Spirit likens God's people to sheep!).

Continually communicate the vision. However, do not implement it until the entire leadership buys into the new vision and direction. Then leaders should share that vision regularly. Talk about it. Pray over it. Play over it.

Finally, empower the people to be active participants in the future vision. Give them authority, not just responsibility. Allow them to be more involved in Kingdom activities (like penetrating the culture with the message) than "church" activities (such as committees and administration). When they see Kingdom results, their nostrils will flare and they will know their labors are worth the effort. They will see they are building the Kingdom, and not a nonprofit organization. Building the Kingdom fires the imagination, quickens the heart, and energizes all our resources.

Other recommendations:

1. *Educate the Congregation on Worship.* In so many churches, little is known about worship. Most think that worship is music and, therefore, the sole province of musicians. Worship is not defined as music in the Bible and it is

surely not assigned to some professional elite squad of worshipers; it is a personal issue. We should all worship privately and publicly. It is the first and greatest commandment in the Old and New Testaments. Teaching on worship will go a long way to bringing the Church into God's presence.

2. *Incorporate the Biblical Traditions of Your History.* There is a renewed interest in the rich tradition of liturgical worship. I would recommend taking a fresh look at the history of your denomination or movement and find its historic, life-giving New Testament worship events that could be incorporated into today's church life. Such things as the way the Eucharist and other ceremonial and sacerdotal observances are celebrated can inform and enrich our contemporary culture.

3. *Restore Awe and Majesty.* Pop cultural worship music tends to be "anthropocentric"—man centered. The lyrics often deal with the feelings and benefits of knowing Christ. Contemporary metaphors and imagery are sometimes thrown in as well. While perhaps helping to make the message relevant, this also tends to keep the songs too earthbound and horizontal. Transcendent songs of worship inspire us with majesty and awe; they contain lyrics of the attributes of God and are often vertical. One additional note: thinking through our prayers (even writing them out) would make our public prayers more powerful.

4. *Keep Christ Central.* Songs about Jesus (and less about what He can do for us) will help keep the worship "Christocentric." Instead of talking only or even primarily about "God," I would recommend speaking more

intimately to Jesus. Every religion has a "Gawd," but Jesus is the center and the reason of our worship.

5. *Increase Congregational Involvement.* This will require reevaluating what occurs in the public service. Ask yourself, *Why is the congregation not involved?* In most cases it is the fault of the leadership. Much of it may be platform driven, and the congregation has been trained to watch. Perhaps they seldom have opportunity to be involved. Do the leaders give them space to participate? Is the music (lyric or melody) too difficult for the congregation to sing? Perhaps simplification is required in some of the events of the worship service. Using a choir as praise leaders, as actual parts of the worship team, will help move the congregation to greater involvement. A new "liturgy" (work of the people) can be vibrant, interactive and participatory.

6. *Increase the Spontaneous.* Keeping a good mixture of form and freedom is critical to the sense of community and involvement. Congregations should feel the freedom at certain parts of the corporate meeting to participate in spontaneous interaction of some kind—prayer, testimony, songs (personal and corporate), the Eucharist, altar ministry and numerous other forms. Just as the Early Church embraced more spontaneous worship, provide (or permit) moments when the service is less structured and the congregation can express, without prompting, their own worship to the Lord.

7. *Encourage Lifestyle Worship.* Worship's relationship with all of life is critical. If, as leaders, we want more of God's presence in our corporate meeting and His action among us, then we must disciple believers as worshipers who don't "do" worship on weekends, but "are" worshipers. The condition of the heart is the

determining factor of lifestyle worship. Style and format are not central to the process of bringing believers into worship; a heart of worship is. If people have a heart for God and a passion for His presence, they will follow any style if the Lord is there.

8. *Seek the Presence of God.* The revealed presence of God should be the center and focus of the corporate gathering—"The LORD your God in your midst, the Mighty One, *[He] will save*" (Zeph. 3:17, *NKJV,* emphasis added). The worship service is not only to retell and memorialize what God has done, but to interact with Him as well.

9. *Become More Culturally Relevant.* Does the worship music represent the ethnic mix of your congregation and community? Do you have plans for training leaders of the ethnic mix of your community? Help your people, your worship team *and yourself* to break out of your cultural cocoon.

10. *Experiment.* In this digital age, we can model the future and check out what it will look like before we get there. With a computer, we can design a car and experience the ride before it is even built. Before we build a new sanctuary for worship, we can go into the future and listen to the acoustics before the foundation is laid. Likewise, we can create a safe environment to creatively experiment. Try new things God shows you in an afternoon or evening session. Experiment with smaller encounters with people, try interactive forms of worship, try new ways of storytelling, and explore reality issues.

Finally, I want to invite you to write me and let me know... See you in the future!

APPENDIX

Many Christians recognize the need to identify and understand how future changes in communication shape the identity of the Church and role of worship among believers. This section is a list of Christian and secular authors I would recommend for further study.

Ambrose, Stephen. *Undaunted Courage.* New York: Simon & Schuster, 1996.

Arn, Charles. "Are Your Paradigms Working for You or Against You?" *Ministry Advantage,* July/August 1996, p. 9.

Bonhoeffer, Dietrich. *Letters and Papers from Prison.* New York: Macmillan, 1971.

Braudel, Fernand. *The Structures of Everyday Life.* New York: Harper & Row Publishers, 1981.

Bridges, William. *Managing Transitions.* Reading, MA: Addison-Wesley Publishing Company, 1991.

Bruce, F. F. *Paul: Apostle of the Heart Set Free.* Grand Rapids: Eerdmans Publishing Company, 1977.

Celente, Gerald. *Trends 2000.* New York: Warner Books, 1997.

Cox, Harvey. *Fire from Heaven: The Rise of Pentecostal Spirituality and the Reshaping of Religion in the Twenty-first Century.* Reading, MA: Addison-Wesley Publishing Company, 1995.

Drucker, Peter. *The New Realities.* New York: Harper & Row Publishers, 1989.

Ellul, Jacques. *The Presence of the Kingdom.* Colorado Springs: Helmers & Howard, 1989.

Fee, Gordon D. *God's Empowering Presence.* Peabody, MA: Hendrickson Publishers, 1994.

Gilder, George. *Microcosm.* New York: Simon & Schuster, 1989.

Gilder, George. *Wealth and Poverty.* New York: Basic Books, Inc., 1981.

Guinness, Os. *The Devil's Gauntlet.* Downers Grove: InterVarsity Press, 1989.

Hendrix, William. *Exit Interviews: Revealing Stories of Why People are Leaving the Church.* Chicago: Moody Press, 1993.

Kennedy, John. *The Torch of the Testimony.* Goleta, CA: Christian Books, 1965.

Lochhead, David. *Theology in a Digital World.* Etobicoke, Canada: United Church Publishing House, 1988.

Mander, Jerry. *Four Arguments for the Elimination of Television.* New York: Morrow Quill Paperbacks, 1978.

McLaren, Brian D. *Reinventing Your Church.* Grand Rapids: Zondervan Publishing House, 1988.

Mead, Loren B. *The Once and Future Church.* Bethesda, MD: The Alban Institute, 1991.

Melnyk, Alexander. "What is Eastern Orthodoxy Anyway?" *Christian History,* vol. 7, no. 2, issue 18, 1988, p. 24.

Morgenthaler, Sally. *Worship Evangelism.* Grand Rapids: Zondervan Publishing House, 1995.

Negroponte, Nicholas. *Being Digital.* New York: Alfred A. Knopf, 1995.

Ong, Walter. *Presence of the Word.* New Haven: Yale University Press, 1967.

Peterson, Eugene. *A Long Obedience in the Same Direction.* Downers Grove: InterVarsity Press, 1980.

Putnam, Robert. "The Strange Disappearance of Civic America." *The American Prospect,* Winter 1996, pp. 1-18.

Rutz, James. *The Open Church: How to Bring Back the Exciting Life of the First Century Church.* Auburn: SeedSowers, 1992.

Snyder, Howard. *The Problem of Wineskins.* Downers Grove: InterVarsity Press, 1975.

Tapscott, Don. *The Digital Economy: Promise and Peril in the Age of Networked Intelligence.* New York: McGraw Hill, 1996.

Thompson, William Irwin. *Coming Into Being.* New York: St. Martin's Press, 1996.

Toffler, Alvin and Heidi. *Creating a New Civilization: The Politics of the Third Wave.* Atlanta: Turner Publishing, 1995.

Verduin, Leonard. *The Reformers and Their Stepchildren.* Grand Rapids: Eerdmans Publishing Company, 1964.

Webber, Robert. *The Complete Library of Christian Worship,* vol. 1. Nashville: Star Song/Abbott Martin, 1994.

———*Worship Is a Verb.* Waco, TX: Word Books, 1985.

Other Books and Resources from LaMar Boschman

The Rebirth of Music

Discover the real meaning and purpose of music.

A Passion for His Presence

Discover what the presence of God is and how to live in His presence dailly.

The Prophetic Song

Understand how the Holy Spirit can sing and play through worshiping believers.

A Heart of Worship

For those looking for worship renewal in their personal life as well as the local church.

Real Men Worship

Discover how to be a real man who is a real worshiper.

Materials available by calling: 1-800-627-0923

For a copy of the Millennium Matrix contact:
Rex Miller at
rexmiller@compuserve.com

Seminars on the subject of this book are available by contacting the author at the address listed below.

Plan now to attend the International Worship Institute. This five-day master worship intensive is held annually in Dallas/Ft Worth, Tx and is attended by hundreds of worship ministers from around the world. Includes over 40 speakers and 120 worshops in all aspects of the worship ministry.

For More Information or a complete catalog contact:
The Worship Institute
PO Box 130
Bedford, Texas 76095
1-800-627-0923
www.worshipinstitute.com